USE IT OR LOSE IT

PATHWAYS TO HEALTHY LIVING

The Incredible, True Adventures of Lew Hollander,
a Senior International Triathlete

By Author Dana Burnett

Copyright   2021 by Author Dana Burnett

First Edition 2021

Produced in the UNITED STATES OF AMERICA
Authored by DANA BURNETT
Designed by EAGLE LADY DESIGN STUDIO
Published by GREEN MANSIONS, INC., LEWIS E. HOLLANDER, JR
P.O. Box 100, Redmond, OR 97756

BOOK COVER:
Photography by KEVIN KUBOTA
Designed by EAGLE LADY DESIGN STUDIO

ISBN 978-1-63901-865-9

BOOKS BY LEWIS E. HOLLANDER:
And Chocolate Shall Lead Us
And Chocolate Shall Lead Us (for children)
Endurance Riding, From Beginning to Winning

For ordering books:
Contact Author Dana Burnett email: dana2@bendbroadband.com
Books also available on Amazon.com
Use It or Lose It also available in ebook

Book Stores and Retail Stores:
Order wholesale directly from IngramSpark

ACKNOWLEDGEMENTS

The list is too long to fully thank everyone for their help in putting this project together. I am particularly grateful to all the athletes, executives, historians, enthusiasts, writers and friends who contributed in one way or another to this amazing project. I thank Lew for sharing his story. It is hoped that Lew's story will inspire those who read it.

– Author Dana Burnett –

CONTENTS

CONTENTS

CONTENTS

CONTENTS

CONTENTS

CONTENTS

RACES

USE IT OR LOSE IT

FORWARD

"Life is not a journey to the grave with the intention of arriving safely in a pretty and well preserved body, but rather to skid in broad-side, thoroughly used up, totally worn out, and loudly proclaiming— 'Wow—What a Ride!"
– Part of the Triathlete's Prayer

There's an acronym for Lew Hollander: WWLD(what would Lew do). There's no question he's always doing something. At 90 there are days when time rolls right off of him and he expects his best days are still to come. Because of what he knows. He's had so many great days in the past people expect his "best" and his "great" to be singular events. "I need a second life," he says. "This one is too busy and too much fun. Love it." Statements like these testify to his love of life and commitment to enjoy every day.

He's a Senior Ironman known around the world. There is perhaps no single human event that teaches us so much about being in our bodies, being at our best, knowing what it really means to be human, than sports. But in this incredibly complex time we're living in, there are not as many role models for healthy and vital aging as there possibly could be.

Lew can accurately be described as an intellectual but at the same time he freely admits that one of his favorite events of all time is the Ride and Tie, where you're down in the "blood and the guts and the mud," where you're one with your horse and your partner and you maybe sprinting long distances if you're one of the great ones, and the record books vouch that he is.

To take the measure of someone like Lew is difficult because he is a singular event, like a star shooting across the sky. As a successful physicist and scientist Lew has spent a lot of his life measuring things so dangerous and tiny that you need equations to adequately explain them. Nuclear radiation instrumentation, a few patents for transducers for audio systems, nano technology and a look into the world of quantum physics.

Lew believes in that mysterious elixir called the "life force" which should not be confused with "the fountain of youth." As a boy he noticed that many of the people he cared about around him were not aging well and he wondered why. He became determined to find out why and to age differently.

He's always asked the big questions, he started asking them over eighty years ago and the answers he came up with have made a difference to him and to others as well. Maybe the answers were there all along but he put them together in a format and became committed to honoring the answers.

In general he's just an active guy. A lot of people live vicariously through their sport's heroes, he observes.

"I would prefer to throw a ball around rather than watch the super bowl."

Historically, it seems that he's always been present on the cutting edge of discoveries. But he is living proof at ninety that his philosophies about health work, backed up by basic principles about daily activity. Given the current state of affairs in the world, health and getting healthier have become major themes. These days anything that isn't right now may seem irrelevant. History can seem irrelevant when the present unfolds as quickly as it does with a digital camera. The now becomes then with a blink of an eye. But aging with integrity and vitality are themes that never seem to get enough attention.

Spirituality and interest in the unknown seem to go hand in hand with great effort and asking big questions. Even Ride and Tie can be seen as a metaphor for life, because your partner disappears and meets challenges and you're supposed to meet ahead and know what to do when you have. Because we all go through changes, we all experience pain and get lost, we all want to be found and feel strong and vital and important. Character and doing your best certainly resonate with Lew. Lew appeared to have burst onto the scene of ultra endurance sports when he completed the Western States 100 at the age of 54.

But he was already a legend in the world of endurance riding and ride and tie, and being a legend takes work.

Lew's friends who knew him recognized that he was a bit of a pioneer, like they all were, pushing at the limits of challenges and enclosures that shouldn't contain them. They were restless, vibrant and with plenty of spirit. Look at the early Western States 100 mile competitors and some of them already knew each other from being Tevis Endurance Ride competitors, because the race basically follows the same course and it had been looming there in some of their minds as a question already. In the words of one world-class athlete who was there, "we were like a family, very accepting of each other's differences." Lew is still in close contact with many of these early friends, no matter how far they've gotten away in miles.

He's got fans around the world. Many times he's appeared at a race, talked to people who didn't have a clue who he was at the time, and then they realized it later. "I had no idea who he was but I certainly did later," said one European fan. "He has been an inspiration ever since." A general definition of the archetypal hero goes something like this—The hero overcomes certain obstacles and achieves certain goals. The hero's main feat is to overcome the monster of darkness. Because of his unusual efforts, Lew has helped to throw light on the monster of aging. Not the only one, certainly, but leading with a kind of cheery example of part of the Triathlete's Prayer. Anything is Possible. If you don't try you have no chance of getting there.

Lew himself is a hard person to measure. He doesn't like to be boxed in. He's got an extremely competitive spirit, and it continues to glow with a special light after being buffeted by the winds of Kona, concussed and battered in New Zealand, and hundreds and hundreds of other body and soul crushing inevitabilities in competition. Lew knows he's got a 30-inch inseam, and in Ride and Tie he'd always be looking for a partner with the same length so they wouldn't waste precious seconds adjusting equipment like stirrup length at the transitions. He considers his specialty to be running up hills, and he still does this practically everyday.

As a scientist he earned an early reputation with inventing patents and formulas with certain crystals and transducers, and with measuring atomic energy through explosions at the higher levels of feasibility. The span of his accomplishments can be intimidating because he's also a writer and a family man. He's got depth, he's given a lot of thought to the meaning of life and the future of mankind, and in addition he's moved into an unofficial, unique role as an ambassador of senior athletics by remaining so healthy and giving off so much encouragement to those he meets around him.

He's like a really fit Santa Claus all year around with the encouragement and good will he spreads to all those who want to be better athletes and indirectly better humans. One might ask what happens spiritually when someone like Lew throws himself out into the extremes of athletic and intellectual challenges so continuously. Is his greatness a palpable thing because he's done it so continually and under so many extreme conditions that he's gotten an answer, only he knows?

He's earned the reputation of an international Ironman who absolutely, unequivocally, does his best no matter what the individual race throws at him. We know the more exercise you get the healthier you are and the more it feeds the brain. But spirit is the characteristic that my ultimately define Lew. It's been a driving force in his life. All the other great accolades just fall in behind...

AUTHOR'S NOTE:

There is no lack of written material on Lew. However, in the bigger picture, a lot of it is fragmented and focusing on only one part of his life. Articles show many sides of Lew, and as a free-lance journalist and writer I had written several articles on him for different publications over about fifteen years. Each time I got the sense that I was only scratching the surface and that he was being polite. I did endurance riding with Lew and family over twenty years ago, and got to see that side of him. And then our paths would cross occasionally. Each time he had done more and made it sound like less.

Finally I said to him, 'someone needs to write a book about your adventures and accomplishments.' He said he'd 'thought about it' and at the time most of his records, articles, photos and personal history seemed to be kept in two large cardboard boxes. This was misleading because he has a huge trophy room.

I said, 'well I can do it,' never thinking he'd take me up on it.

We started five years ago and got a really rough manuscript which only scratched the surface of his life's work and philosophies. Then the project was halted and it seemed like the project was put on a permanent hold. But in the spring of 2020 he emailed me and asked if I'd like to try tackling it again. I said "of course," but this time around I didn't take short cuts, or as few as I could considering the time limit we were working under. It's not often that a writer gets a chance to write about a person like Lew, who has lived such a big life and given so much to so many people. No one wants to be defeated, and Lew's message is that there is a simple and very clear way to fight aging.

One of my high school science teachers used to look at our class with mock scorn and mumble something in a good natured way about idle blobs of protoplasm with the implication that we the class were teetering on the precipice. Ever since then the description has stuck in my mind. That some of us couldn't or wouldn't make full use of either our physical or intellectual potential. Happily, Lew never followed a standard series of expectations about anything and has always pushed the limits of what is possible, suggesting to others that they can do the same even if it's just one step at a time.

One theme that appears over and over again in Lew's message is just a reminder that we already know—daily exercise is great and not only contributes to our physical and emotional well-being but to our intellectual capabilities as well.

USE IT OR LOSE IT. A simple idea.

Lew's message is that there is a better way to live and fight aging than many people are aware of. Maybe they've just forgotten it. Go Hard! Live Long! Lew's training methods are sound and backed up by the medical evidence. It does need to be noted however, that non-athletes need to consult with a doctor before beginning any program. In addition, individual athletes all aspire to reach higher levels and each are unique, so when in doubt, they should consult a doctor as well. The strength of Lew's character has made him into the Ironman that he is today.

"We all operate aerobically or die. To improve athletic performance I say 'go anaerobic everyday," Lew explains. "That means you are using more oxygen than you can breathe in so obviously you cannot sustain that for very long. So why do it? Because it pushes the body to its limit and it encourages hormones, muscle and bone to grow and strengthen and extend your anaerobic threshold so you can perform longer at the extreme level," Lew states. "There are no down sides to this that I'm aware of except you live longer, stronger and keep your energy level higher. Your heart may adapt and change a little. The key is if you start you can not quit—that is when you get into trouble."

His story is hoped to inspire and show the possibilities that can come with a commitment to healthy and vital living, not as the total answer for any individual's health plan.

"Lot's of people are good at things but they wander off," Lew observes. "I persist." Two words rarely crop up in Lew's vocabulary. "Tired" and "Pain." They just don't come up in conversation with Lew. Which leads one back to his philosophy that the toughest races are won with over ninety per cent mental commitment. And of course, life is the biggest race anyone will ever get to compete in.

So once again I get the feeling that I have only scratched the surface on Lew and that he's still being polite, but I like this story. And I am reminded constantly of one of Lew's favorite sayings credited to John Barrymore. "A man is not old until regret takes the place of his dreams."

– Author Dana Burnett

Disclaimer: Anyone embarking on a new exercise program should consult a physician first. The personal views expressed in this book are the subject's views only, and need to be appreciated as that.

CHAPTER 1

THE TRIATHLETE'S PRAYER: ANYTHING IS POSSIBLE

Lew Hollander was on the fast track for success the day he was born. He probably came out thinking "Go Anaerobic" but couldn't quite verbalize it until a few years later. Lew is now a famous guy, responsible for inspiring athletes of all ages around the world to keep pushing it. To "Use It Or Lose It."

"It" is the life force in the amazing human body. Now more than ever, we realize how important Lew's message is. Google him on the internet and you will see his accomplishments as a legendary Ironman, Endurance Rider, noted Physicist and Author. But it takes awhile to get to know him. There's the athlete, and there's the thinker, and the deeper you dig the harder it becomes to try to separate one from the other. And he has become lower key about his accomplishments the more he has collected. Those who know him tend to describe him as great and humble at the same time. But there's no doubt he has a lot of confidence. There are themes that resonate and repeat in his life and it's all about persistence, achievement, doing your best everyday, and personal honesty. Self-knowledge comes along as a by-product of sticking to core values.

"I believe we are part of a far greater system or endeavor," he says. "We all have our role. We belong here. I believe if there is spirit, after life, God or whatever you wish to call it, it will be best found INSIDE OF EACH OF US. Not told by priests, clerics, etc. If you want the answers, look within."

In the hustle and flow of everyday living, there maybe days when you're burned out, when you feel like we've all been cloned from some spiritless master plan and the same universal script is just going to repeat itself endlessly while the oceans continue to rise, pandemics savage the world, and other inconvenient truths manifest themselves. So it's nice to know that someone out there has broken the mold and reinvented it, laid down his own track, and rewritten aging stereotypes by putting a spin on it that most people find hard to believe.

On his ninetieth birthday Lew completed a sprint triathlon in a virtual race in the area around his house.

The fact that I can do this is miraculous, he says. "There will always be those greater than you and those less than you," he states. But the most important person you have to account to is yourself. When you fail to try, it's worse than losing.

Lew Hollander is a natural phenomena, a mercurial presence, an intellectual power and an inspiring athlete who has few if any equals. And that's just on a good day. Lew turned 90 in June of 2020. He's been famous a long time for different reasons but loved and respected because he defies the odds. Whoever thought he would become one of the outspoken champions for senior athletes? It doesn't matter. He is.

"Success does not come to you—you go to it." And to that end Lew has courted success with the same amount of dedication and commitment that it might have taken Christopher Columbus to find America. Lew has found something that is really big. You're going to have to read the whole book to find out. And remember, that sometimes when you get out on the really, really long trails and you lose your sense of direction and think you can't take another step, that maybe exactly when you actually find yourself. But you have to battle with the feeling of being lost, before you rediscover who you are and who you really want to become.

At 90 Lew continues to inspire everyone around him with his commitment to going hard, living long, and doing it with class and style as a really unique athlete and human being. How did this Ironman get so much Iron in his backbone? Lew was born back in New York in 1930 into a flourishing family right before the Great Depression hit. Family finances would change over a period of time and dictated that Lew go from private to public school. It was then that Lew began to understand the theory of the survival of the fittest with new kids. His father, the original Lew, taught his son how to fight back when he got bullied. Occasionally, Lew Jr. experimented with chemicals and blew up things, and studied order and patterns in science. He began to understand the feeling of empowerment resulting from understanding how pieces of the world fit together. And maybe over the years he wanted to help other people understand how to put the pieces together for healthy living. It's a step-by-step, day-by-day commitment.

As a young boy Lew became confidant that there was a way to age, and a way not to age, based on what he saw around him. The best and most positive way to age would become his life long goal. It could be said that mankind has a universal search for spirituality and wholeness that takes many different forms. Certainly aging and what goes along with it form some of the most difficult questions. Everyone wants that magic pill to roll it back, to have it not go so fast forward. Like a legendary hero of sorts, Lew has done the battle with aging and shed some light. In the midst of the battle he was able to ask some questions and pursue the answers, and so bring a type of healing for anyone who is interested.

In his own words he was bright and sensitive as a boy and people noticed his focus.

Eighty years later he has become known as a man who has helped recalibrate the bar on getting older. He is a hard-working man who is willing to share his experiences and ideas about healthy living and aging in a way that is real, and vibrant, and easy to understand. He was always an athlete who enjoyed sports and riding, in his own words 'not that extra special at any of it,' until he matured into an adult whose zest for life took him on a series of adventures which are still evolving.

Lew considers The Western States One Hundred Mile Foot Race in the

High Sierras to re-birthing him into a different mind set and new skin, coming down the birth canal of the grueling one hundred mile race a slightly different version of the same person he was before he started. Defenses torn down, body destroyed, but definitely enjoying the scenery and the battle. Never lonely because there was so much pain. It's said that the only thing ordinary about this race is that it starts.

It's possible that Ironmen are wired differently. They maybe getting a blister that's bigger than anything they've ever seen before, running with tendonitis or a kidney stone coming on, but they push through until they can't push anymore. Lew has worn that legacy well. Some would say to extremes, but other Ironmen say he will make the best out of any race, regardless of the conditions.

"The only time I ran long for training was for the Western States," he recalled. "I had some 6 hour days around Grey Butte (Central Oregon).

"...Pat Browning and some other fanatical endurance riding friends were running long distances and talking about the Western States Run," he recalls in a section from his book "Endurance Riding-From Beginning to Winning." At this time I had not even run a 10k (ten thousand meters or 6.3 miles), but I dreamed of running the Western States. Little by little, I began to run, using all the same rules I had established from endurance riding. By 1978, I ran the Portland Marathon, I realized it was the same(idea), one step at a time. You have to do with what you've got. All my years of endurance riding were PERFECT training for running long distances. I was mentally prepared and knew what it took to train myself. Being a middle of the pack runner, I learned the joy and meaning of, "To Compete is To Win."

My hero, Pat Fitzgerald, ran the Western States. I thought perhaps there was a chance, and I sent in my own entry during a rash moment in 1983. They were smart enough not to accept me. I tried again in 1984, and catastrophe struck. They accepted me!..."

The Western States race starts at Squaw Valley California early in the morning near the site of the 1960 Winter Olympics. The finish line is in Auburn California 100.2 miles away and the runners will jog through wilderness that is just waiting for them to make a mistake and wimp out. Everything Lew thought he knew from tough marathon races in his previous experience and from endurance riding and ride and tie got redefined as his will propelled him forward while his body screamed for him to stop. Repeatedly. Fortunately for Lew, he gets better with the battle.

In his Endurance book he compares the challenge to "…having a tiger by the tail! It was simply impossible to do this at 54 years of age, having never done a lot of running. I took inventory. What have I got? I know the trail; I am tough in rough terrain. Because of endurance riding I am well trained for long duration events of 15 to 30 hours in length. I am not a fast runner, but I am steady and can keep going. I dropped everything else and used all my skills as an endurance rider to train myself. I qualified at Skagit Ultra-50 miler, which required 50 miles in less than ten hours. I barely made the 50 miles on flat roads, and I thought, "How can I go twice as far in tough terrain?" Desire is everything in an athlete. The want to, the drive, the willingness to crawl on busted glass, broken bones, puking, hallucinating, whatever it takes just to get to the finish line because in the really tough races the finish line beckons like a cruel phantom and the closer it gets the more unreachable it seems. To survive as an ultra athlete takes a conditioned body and lots of focus, and Lew has had the focus part down from an early age. He recalls that when he was in first grade, the principal of the school named Mrs. Wing studied him and wrote a PhD thesis on him because his ability to focus impressed her so deeply.

Driven, driving, determined, the alliterations can go on forever but while Lew was running the Western States 100 at the age of 54 he really knew he could survive it because of his experiences as an endurance rider. A love of riding that began when he was a little boy and eventually took him to national and international recognition in that field alone.

"… (When) Race day arrived and I was at the starting line at 5.a.m as I had done many times before. It was different this time because there was no horse," Lew recalled in a section from his book. "I was scared and thinking, "Hey, you have the wrong person out here, there must be some mistake. A shout rang out and we all found ourselves running up the familiar trail to Emigrant Gap, sliding, slipping, clawing, crawling, through the snow, over the top, down the narrow trail where I always have trouble passing other horses, but no problem now...."

"This is fun, this is fun?" Lew recalls trying to convince himself while following the Western States Trail Course. The Western States Historic Trail forces runners to climb 18,000 feet and then descend nearly 23,000 feet before reaching the relative sanctuary of the Placer High School in Auburn, California at the end. Athletes have the fire and the ice, the ability to withstand an unbelievable amount of physical discomfort and at the same time have stoic emotional strength. What happened to Lew on the course? He realized that a lot of so-called limits had green lights blinking in front of them if you could push past sore muscles and negative thinking.

"As I ran I gained an insight about myself," he recalls. Spiritual growth can occur when you're pushing the limits of who you think you are. But then there are the practical considerations of surviving a race like Western States. Can your pride survive if you quit? Will your body survive if you don't? But there is one theme which resonates throughout Lew's story. He will throw it down, he will throw out the challenge, to himself, to go just one step further.

Two days before the race began he arrived for Indoctrination Meetings. He had gotten a ticket in based on his wide athletic qualifications. One of the biggest threats on the race is dehydration if nothing else happens. Lew estimates that he drank 60 gallons of water during the race, which kept his 160-pound frame hydrated. Such small details as keeping feet from overheating become big. Ice water, Vaseline, a change of running shoes and new socks make a big difference. Having the support of a good crew at the check-points is huge.

CHAPTER 1   THE TRIATHLETE'S PRAYER

Lew's daughter Heather would meet Lew at the aid stations and guide him to the crew area. There is a doctor at each stop who checks you out, according to Lew. At Michigan Bluff the doctor asked him what his name was and he answered. But when asked where he was from Heather had to answer "Oregon" for him. The doctor said "Oregon?" like that explained a lot and let Lew move on.

CHAPTER 2

THIS IS FUN?

Lew was the 230th finisher out of 385 men and women who started Western States 100 mile endurance run on July 7th and 8th, 1984. Two hundred and fifty people completed it. He was familiar with the course in the sense that he'd already ridden and finished the renowned Tevis Endurance Ride three times. There were many times during the race when he had the "this is fun?" dialogue with himself. He was 54. He had already crossed a lot of finish lines but Western States was different. Lew had decided to wage his own war against passive and undignified aging when he was only a kid.

There were a lot of misconceptions and stereotypes floating around about the so-called Golden Years then and some would say there still are now. It could be that there was the loss of one person in particular, an athlete who stopped exercising, who Lew carries forever in his own heart. At any rate, he considers himself an ordinary person but leaves out the part where it's concluded he does extraordinary things.

He'd been on the planet over half a century already when he entered and completed Western States, but time is relative for some. It could be that all the laws in physics informed him that it was better to stay in motion. As for aging—"It's all in your head," he says. But obviously, he'd put in the miles and earned the golden ticket to one of the most elusive and prestigious endurance events around, The Western States. As beautiful as it is tough. As tough as it is beautiful. He and his former wife Hanne had "cleaned house" in most major equine endurance events for years.

Maybe he was up to reinvent his limits. He knew that he wanted to test his limits and all the endurance riding and marathon running in his background had made him want to push the limits just a little more. One of Lew's secrets is the discipline to achieve his goals. Once he sets his sights on a goal and narrows in on it the goal doesn't fight back. The insight that he gained during the Western States race was that his potential was going to be redefined. He has said frequently that his greatest thoughts come to him when he's running and that questions get answered. But on the Western States One Hundred the geography of the course is the ultimate truth tester, pushing the limits of what you thought you were, reinventing your personal reality.

"One of my strengths I think is that I have a lot of fast twitch muscles which makes me a good sprinter and strangely enough a good long distance runner. All in between 1, 5k, 10k, ½ marathon and even full marathons," he explains. "A good runner has all slow twitch muscles but when they are used up he is done. Fast twitch can recover quickly and I get a second wind."

Endurance events do tend to test what's best in a person and weed out what is weak. There's a polite disclaimer on one description of Western States. "Entry should not be taken lightly." We're off to see the wizard in Auburn over 100 miles away, if the bear, cougar, rattlesnakes, blisters, and dehydration don't get you along the way. Western States is rated as the mother of all tough races in the country.

The sheer appalling difficulty of it, the unrelenting drama of the trail and everything that can go wrong, makes it miraculous that so many things can go right. Completion of the race proved many of Lew's theories, mainly that the human body is capable of so much more than it is generally given credit for, especially since the age of leisure came to town. Temperatures on the race can range from 20 to 110, and since many run into the night and the next day, two flashlights are required.

Emigrants Pass, Granite Chief Wilderness, followed by the canyons of the California gold country, punctuated with the crossing of the main stem of the Middle Fork of the American River. Sure there are people cheering you on, watching out for you, but they can't do it for you. It's got to come from the inside. When exhaustion seems like a full-time companion and you can't remember your name, when the endorphins have flown away to roost somewhere else, the historic trails of homesteaders and prospectors lead you home. Only home never really feels quite the same because you've been off to see the wizard and found out the wizard really lies in you.

Because in all the grit and sweat and blistering exertion of Western States Lew wanted the finish line bad enough. He wanted a revelation that he could do more, be more, live more. Proving to himself and others that he was going to continue to push boundaries on aging and the stereotypes that went along with the old ideas. As an active and legendary Ride and Tie participant, Lew used the strategies of that sport to help him through the tougher parts of the Western States. But will and spunk towed him in the really tougher places. At 74 miles he reached a dark point where it also happened to be dark. He saw a sign written by somebody with a twisted sense of humor.

"Congratulations, Only One More Marathon to Go." It was his new day, his first birthday of a different era and he still feels that way from the viewpoint at ninety. But after Western States he was ready for a new goal and he found it in the idea of the Hawaii Ironman, where the best compete against the best and may wonder why they keep coming back. The Western States One Hundred became a pivotal experience for Lew. It would launch him and propel him forward, and help coalesce everything he'd developed in endurance riding minus the horse, leading him into an entirely different global arena. At ninety today, he looks back almost forty years later, crediting Western States with giving him the confidence and sharpening his desire to excel in one of the most grueling sports available.

Triathlon would become his next great epic adventure and ongoing challenge combining swimming, biking and running. It's said that one of the goals of the triathlete is to say "what a ride!" at the end of the engagement. Not to arrive in a body that's never been used. Coincidentally, the body that's really been used will have a much longer run in the overall engagement of life even if a few battle scars have been accrued along the way. It's a sound investment.

Lew was born to go anaerobic, a nifty little word he uses to describe the body's renewal process. He has collected a formidable array of little black statues to commemorate 22 years at Kona. Along the way he has blazed a path for senior athletes and all athletes who want to go harder, longer. The senior years, according to Lew, are not the years to give up on your dreams.

CHAPTER 3

LEW'S TIMELINE

The competitive spirit burns brightly in the driven athletes. Maybe there are times when one feels like eviscerating the competition, but by and large it seems most great athletes come to realize they are competing against time and against competition in a much larger sense than the watch. How good can they get, without excuses, without quitting? How far can they push? And if you're really up for a challenge you compete against what maybe your own personal best that was yesterday. Along with many others Lew is credited with being a bit of a pioneer in his age group. He was in on the front line with many cutting edge scientific inventions, and he was on the front line in many ultra endurance events as they evolved.

Perhaps it's been the way he's done it that has made him so revered. Giving encouragement, setting an example, just doing his best over and over.

He's been pushing time, doing time, marching to his own drummer in his own inimitable fashion. Which translates over and over into "Do Your Best."

Lew was born June 6th, 1930.

"My mother was an Irish Catholic and my father was third generation German-Dutch-Jewish," he explains. One of the nuns carried him in to meet his mother and said there was a sign, a sign that he was going to be a great person. You have to ask him about that yourself. "So maybe someday I will be important," he observes, "but it better hurry up because I am running out of time."

Lew seems unaware of the positive impact he's had on people all around the world, people who know he's an inspiration. Sister Madonna Buder of Seattle, Washington, has carved out her own unique spot in the world of Triathlon legends. She has been tabbed "The Iron Nun," for competing in the many Ironman distance races for so many years.

"Lew and I have a long history of competing in the same events," she observes. "Lew Hollander seems to thrive on challenges. His drive appears unlimited and is exhibited in both his mental and physical endeavors. His enthusiasm for life is infectious, which he willingly shares with others through kindly advice and encouragement. Since both he and I have apparently outgrown our competition we seem to be complementing each other in the drive to continue moving FORWARD despite AGE! Opening the 90 age group is the goal!"

Fans have watched Lew for years, marveling at how time seems to have been so kind. Others fear that like the legend of Icarus, he might have flown too close to the sun, but he has debunked a lot of myths by observing simple truths. I reflect constantly on the fact that I'm alive, he says. I've never been the fastest but I'm usually the oldest at a race and that means something to me. Online sources state that moderate to high levels of exercise are correlated to reducing or slowing aging by reducing inflammatory properties of the body.

For centuries legends have explored the idea of drinking from a magic cup that provides miraculous powers, like happiness or eternal youth, where the drinker is promised the abundance of infinite sustenance. As it turns out, steady intelligent exercise will begin to feel like drinking out of a magic cup. The body will say "thank-you" in very special ways.

Exercise promotes an overall sense of well-being by improving strength, slowing aging, building muscle, weight loss, along with multiple other attributes such as increasing cardiovascular fitness and boosting immunity. Besides that, it's just Fun! Lew stresses that going anaerobic everyday is not for the non -athlete, and that anyone who's embarking on a serious exercise program should consult with a doctor first.

There are notable days on Lew's timeline. Some are private, having to do with family and special times that are meant to be private.

He has 6 children, 3 grand kids, and 3 great grand kids.

But his athletic career is marked by huge accomplishments that are notable on certain years and certain times of the year. Prior to his entrance into Ironman Lew was a champion endurance rider, among other things. In 1974, 1983, and 1985 he completed the Historic and Legendary Tevis Cup 100 mile ride from Tahoe to Auburn. In 1975 he completed the Ochoco 150 mile endurance ride in 19 hours and 30 minutes to win.

1984 was a banner year because it marked his completion of Western States. 1985 started his heroic relationship with the Hawaii Ironman in October.

In 1979 Lew was inducted into the American Endurance Riding Hall of Fame.

Lew's accomplishments in the ITU (International Triathlon Union) have been quite solid. He has won ITU World Championships six times. Lew won 2 gold medals at the Nike World Masters in 1998 in Portland, Oregon. He has raced the Hawaii Ironman a staggering 25 times but could not make the time cut-off at age 84 and 85. He had the fastest time in Hawaii for over 80 with fifteen hours and 48 minutes. He set the fastest time for over 70 at the Florida Ironman finishing in 12 hours and 58 minutes.

Lew's timeline is so full of achievements that it's hard to believe that what's put out here in this book is not a complete record. When he was doing what he was doing, racing all over the world, he wasn't that interested in writing every event down. It's just been like one ongoing, gigantic exploration of the life force in Lew.

Everybody knows those big years didn't just happen. Those big years on Lew's timeline are so bright because of inestimable work, dedication, luck, ability and perseverance.

Lew was two-time Hawaii Ironman World Champion in 2010 and 2011. In 2013 he was voted USA Triathlon All American and also Ironman All World Athlete. He was awarded Performance of the Year by Ironman in 2012.

If ever there was a person who understood pivotal moments it's Lew. The year 2015 was disappointing in some respects to Lew, but a new door opened when an old one appeared to close. He was invited to Bahrain in December of 2015 to do the ½ Ironman in December. And then in January of 2016 he returned to Dubai to compete in another race. His Royal Highness Sheik Nasser of Bahrain extended these invitations to Lew who was given the "royal treatment" each time. But the idea behind these invitations for Lew to compete was to help illustrate or show what senior athletes are capable of. And so while it began clear that certain parts of Lew's athletic career would be changing he slowly stepped into another evolution as the senior athlete who shows what older age can be like.

As a scientist Lew knows how to connect the dots, but as a human he realizes that life is life, and the more success you want to have in it, the more you have to look at the understated and overstated signs along the way. Like if you don't use the rudder you'll hit the rocks. With a Boy Scout smile and down to earth charm you might be surprised to know that Lew enjoyed creating mini explosions in his lab when he was a kid. Since then he's been creating different kinds of explosions just by his presence.

It's like he and a lot of his friends raised a different kind of flag on territory that wasn't even marked when they started doing all their ultra endurance events. It was a celebration of life, of being alive, of being fit and not afraid to test the horizons. Imagine a game TV show host, getting his audience psyched up. He leans forward eagerly into the spotlight and asks the twenty five million dollar question. "How many of you would like to be active at 80?"

And it's not a trick question, an infomercial or a threat. It's just a question. Because the question already implies that you might not be that active at 80, that you may in fact feel lucky if you can get out of the rocking chair to walk around the block. Older age. Shrouded in a fog of dulled expectations, misinformation, lack of leadership, cliché stereotypes, and withering hope. Who could be out running the Hawaii Ironmen at 80 and set a record? Who would want to? Lew. The rocking chair is not magical. It doesn't take you anywhere. You're stuck in one spot. In his own unique, march to his own drummer way, Lew has recalibrated the bar on aging for anyone who's interested enough to think about the subject with an open mind.

Because with as many technological and medical evolutions as there have been, perhaps there has not been enough pro-active work done on getting people healthy from the beginning and keeping them there. So they would truly understand what the human body is capable of. Some of us wander through our days, wishing we could be on a game show and win some fancy big prize, bask in the spotlight, but perhaps we're missing the biggest prize of all, which is just to work harder at being healthy. What bigger reward could there be than health combined with the idea that old age doesn't have to be quite so limited?

Lew's biggest secret is his lack of a secret. IT takes conscious effort to be healthy and strong whether you want to be an Ironman or an everyday speed walker. For Lew staying in shape was never a choice. It was a specific commitment from the time he was a boy. "There's no secret to staying in shape," Lew repeats patiently. "You have to work hard, eat right and go anaerobic everyday." There are wise investments, and there are wise investments. It's not selfish to invest in your health. Anything is possible. That's the triathlete's prayer. It opens up whole new vistas. A good, healthy, long life is like money in the bank in more ways than one. Lew is known in the world of ultra endurance events and even more people are getting to know him through his connections with healthy senior advocacy.

According to online sources, sedentary or inactive lifestyle increases all causes of mortality, doubling the risk of many diseases. Along with all that scary stuff, most people just feel better when they get into a regular exercise program and stick with it.

Personally, Lew feels that the moment when you have pushed yourself to the limit, wonderful things happen to your endocrine system, which helps to integrate and control the glandular output of adrenals, pituitary, thyroid, parathyroid, ovaries and testes. These are all awakened and start producing again.

"We are designed to die at 30 to 35," Lew believes, "and the endocrine system starts shutting down to accomplish this end. This is called aging. This was essential to the cave man days as the community could not afford to house and feed nonproductive members."

The competitive spirit can be a two-edged sword. But over a lifetime Lew's passion has burned brightly enough that people can see it at a distance.

"This is living," Lew says cheerfully from his perspective as a ninety years old who completed a sprint triathlon on his 90th birthday in June of 2020. "It's all an expression of me living, of the life force, and if you want to look at the benefits of exercise versus the downside, the downside is very little."

CHAPTER 4

A LEAGUE OF HIS OWN

Lew has made the Pacific Northwest his playground and honed his skills on the rivers, mountains and plains of challenging terrain. As has been said, Central Oregon in particular makes a great haven for Ironmen. The often extreme weather has prepared Lew for extreme races all over the world. Lew has carved out a singular niche for himself in the areas he's competed in. The accolades and awards are nice but the respect is probably the biggest honor. The love is a by-product of seeing a man perform against all odds, make it look easy, and send that out as his legacy and challenge for future generations.

And while Central Oregon cannot take credit for producing an athlete of Lew's caliber, it is clear that he has flourished in this rugged environment that seems to breed athletes. Train here--go there. Hand-picking competitions around the country and across the world. "If I need to take a vacation I just see where the races are," he remarks casually. His box of newspaper clippings and certificates speak more of his accomplishments than he is likely to.

In 2004 he won the Pilot Butte challenge, an uphill race that lives up to its name. He took first in his age group at the age of 74, and sprinted back down while everyone else was catching their breath. He won the Grizzly Mountain Ride and Tie Championship. Competed in the Kona Ironman with a finishing time of fifteen hours, forty-seven minutes and 39 seconds. Sandwiched somewhere in between, just to stretch his legs out, he ran in the Hot Shot 10K run in Prineville with son Lewis, with a blistering time of 50 minutes and 24 seconds.

Looking at Lew's statistics 2004 wasn't a particularly busy year but he still squeezed in the San Diguieto ½ marathon which he considered to be a "tough course" in two hours and two minutes. Followed by the Dirty Half ½ marathon and then the San Diego ½ marathon in a sizzling two hours and 42 seconds. The ability to combine business with pleasure, see friends and travel the world have made his life rich. He's an American son, a universal traveler, and a deep thinker. "Slow and steady does win a race," he believes. "If you don't quit, if you do persist, if you train yourself mentally and physically so that you do cross the finish line." To finish is to win.

Part of Lew's training program has always included training within training for specific events. And for fun. For example, he has competed in many Biathlon events. Biathlon includes cycling and running competitions at distances such as 5K-40k-10K or some combination. He competed in the Summer Games in the early nineties, the Firecracker in Portland in 1991 and 1992, the Mazama twice in 1991, then in 1997 and 1999.

He competed in the RoseFest Tanisbourne in 1990, 1991, 1992, 1993, 1994 and 1999. The Midsummer race in 1989 and 1991, the Bend Biathlon in 1995, the Road Warrior Kan-Nee-Ta in 1999, and the Fresh Air Sports Duathlon Series. Twice in 2005 and once in 2006. He competed twice in the Bend Bike and Sport Time Trials in 2006 and the Sunrise to Summit Duathlon in 2006 and 2007. But as Lew admits he does not write down everything since he's more interested in doing it then writing about it afterwards.

Greg Pressler, of Why Racing Events in Seattle, has known Lew since the 1990's.

"Lew is a remarkable man," he observed, when asked how he sees Lew. "I've known him since we competed in many of the same events back in the 1990's. As a guy with a technical background, Lew has been known for his methodical, "head down" approach to racing. Other athletes observed how he always seemed to have the details of racing down to a "t," a skill that meshes well with the detailed nature of triathlons. While many aging athletes slow with age, Lew seemed to get faster, hitting his stride as he hit his 70's! Lew's influence extends well beyond the borders of the triathlon transition zone.

He continues to be a gracious international ambassador of multi-sport racing, the pursuit of healthy lifestyles, and the role of older athletes in sport. He is always willing to share his stories and memories of competition, a precious gift to younger athletes. And lest you think a ninety year old is slow, Lew will prove you wrong. He can still embarrass other competitors who fail to adequately prepare for a race!"

Lew is a scientist. As a scientist and physicist he participated in many atomic bomb tests while in the Navy. He worked at the U.S. Naval Radiological Defense Laboratory in San Francisco, California from April 1955 to April 1957 in the areas of radiological defense, nuclear weapons testing and instrumentation. He received a high note of excellence in a letter from a Captain in the U.S. Navy when he was getting ready to move on: "I am taking this opportunity, now that the formalities of your separation from active duty are completed, to express my personal appreciation for the high quality of the professional work and services you have rendered this Laboratory during the past three years.

"Your excellent understanding of the problems of radiation measurement and control is evidenced by the outstanding performance of the apparatus you have designed and assembled. The equipment is of such high accuracy and stability that it is used as a standard against which all types of atomic radiation instruments are checked and calibrated

"It was especially gratifying to me to note that all of your projects at the Laboratory have been well planned, organized, and methodically executed. An example of this was your supervision of the design and fabrication of a very useful high voltage measuring system. This assignment involved an initial investigation of suitable solutions, a difficult procurement problem for essential components and a detailed engineering design phase. The officers and employees of this Laboratory join me in wishing you every success in whatever activities you may undertake in civilian life.

I also hope that you will endeavor to maintain an appropriate connection with the U.S. Naval Reserve, as I am sure that organization would profit by your support and participation in its program."

But many of his less well-known achievements deserve meritorious observation as well. "It's difficult to measure high voltage," he observes. He studied at the National Bureau of Standards to learn from Dr. Day, a teacher he described as "being the best." The x-ray beam that he developed was capable of measuring 300,000 volts. Over fifty volts can harm a human because of the flow so safety standards become of paramount importance. The National Bureau of Standards was established by Congress in 1901 as an authoritative domestic measurement and standards laboratory and was the first federal science research lab of the federal government.

One of Lew's recent inventions is a chemical compound to put fires out without a lot of firefighters. He is credited with having 22 US Patents. "Currently I am engaged in research on Molecular Nano Technology using rutile as a substrate," he says. From his perspective, working as a Naval Officer stationed at the Naval Radiological Defense Laboratory was his first real exposure to a scientific career.

"...At that time I found a nuclear radiation sensitive crystal, Cadmium Sulfide, CdS, and developed a method to grow these crystals. I did research in semiconductors, piezoresistivity, photoconductivity and related fields. I did considerable work on Rutile, Titanium Dioxide, $TiO2$... I have numerous, reviewed scientific papers in the American Physical Society Journals such as Physical Review, Journal of Applied Physics, The Review of Scientific Instruments, Journal of the Acoustic Society, and many, many other technical journals," Lew states. "I am listed in Marquis Who's Who in Science and Engineering 2000-2001 and the Millennium Edition of Who's Who in the World. I was a partner in Integrated Transducers Inc., Guaynabo, Puerto Rico and President of Green Mansions Inc., PO Box 11, Redmond, Oregon 97756."

Lew has always asked the big questions, and one question that's kind of difficult to answer is what happens when scientists and doctors can keep humans alive longer. Lew has spent his whole life developing a program for that question about quality of life, integrity, and enjoyment of life. Joy is a necessary commitment to healthy living. People actually sign up for races just to be with him, even though it's harder now in virtual reality times. He is a positive ambassador of the now, who embraces the difficulties in life and keeps racing with them.

Dave Scott is the first US Triathlete to win the Hawaii Ironman Triathlon Championship six times. This legendary Ironman had some valuable observations about Lew when asked to comment.

"I'll offer what is certainly parallel to most admirers of Lew. Lew is a remarkable athlete and an extraordinarily humble man. My recollection is that our paths crossed at the Ironman(Kona) sometimes in the late 80's when he was just getting started in his Ironman career. During his racing career he has defied the aging myths and mastered the Ironman at the World Championships. I know he held the world record until recently when a Japanese athlete claimed the title as the oldest finisher. Probably the most noteworthy characteristic about Lew's legacy is his sincere humble demeanor. He always has an infectious spirit and radiant smile for all athletes. His positive reflection is emblematic for his enthusiasm and zest for life. I was honored to race with him and also share his victories, seeing him cross the finish line many times at Kona."

Tim Yount, Chief Sport Development Officer for USA Triathlon, and 30 year Team USA Manager, has known Lew awhile:

"I have known Lew for nearly my entire 30 years at USAT. From competing at National Championships where anything less than gold was missing the goal to his representation on Team USA where he won many podium finishes to Ironman which is where he really set himself apart, Lew might be one of the all time greats who will leave his legacy in many areas of the sport. Even today at 90, he is as revered as when he was in his seventies," Tim Yount observed.

And while Lew holds high standards of discipline in his training combined with healthy amounts of talent and work, it is worth noting that his early championship years in the sport of Endurance Riding and Ride and Tie helped pave the way for his success in other sports later on.

Kathleen A. Henkel, Executive Director of the American Endurance Ride Conference(AERC), was able to contribute a few of her thoughts on Lew's accomplishments in Endurance Riding. "AERC was incorporated in 1972 and Lew is a lifetime member of the organization, along with his family members and he was one of the very first members of AERC's Board of Directors. As such he was responsible for some of AERC's early rules and sharing input regarding AERC's bylaws. Lew and his (second) wife Hanne were very active members and rode many miles in the early years along with their children."

Lew and Hanne were inducted into the AERC Hall of Fame in 1979. Lew wrote a book regarding endurance, titled "Endurance Riding—From Beginning to Winning," imparting many of his strategies related to the sport of endurance. Lew's number in the AERC was 792. He introduced the rider mileage program and coined the phrases "complete is to win," and "to finish is to win."

It's hard to measure what Lew gave to the sport of Endurance riding.

He introduced the "Vet Gate" concept used all over the world today, and was instrumental in developing the AERC Best Condition Form, and many other innovations which shaped the sport. In 1973 he was AERC Reserve National Champion on Prince Kosarm. He was ranked 4th place in the AERC in 1974, 7th place in 1978, 25th place in 1976 and winner of over 100 wins and Best Condition awards in endurance and ride and tie. Lew has ridden over 9181 miles(per AERC records) plus several thousand ride and tie miles and most of those finishes were in the top ten.

CHAPTER 5

A POWERFUL LOVE (MEET ME IN OCTOBER)

Lew has called the Hawaii Ironman "the toughest, ugliest race" he's ever done and for over 24 years he would go back in October and engage in the same kind of physical dialogue with the elements and the mileage. The island challenge doesn't give it up easily. The best of the best, giving it their best, and still sometimes having a very difficult time finishing. Head winds, side winds, ocean currents, dehydration—it's been called the mother of all Ironman Challenges with respectful awe.

In the narrative of Lew's personal history Kona has been an epic narrative. An open water swim of 2.4 miles in strong currents, a bike ride of one hundred and twelve miles with winds that like toying with humans, and then the marathon run. The rules and guidelines within this Ironman don't appear to have a lot of flexibility. Participants must finish the swim/cycle portion within ten hours and thirty minutes, and cross the finish line within sixteen hours and fifty minutes to have completed officially. The winds on the cycle portion can help make or break a competitor. Usually they're fiercely unhelpful and only once in awhile are they calm.

At Kona you're in the company of super stars who are world-class athletes. Many of them have extremely inspirational stories of their own, of triumph over heartache and disaster. It's a cliché to say it's a triumph of the human spirit because that cliché is bounced around a lot but Kona really is a lot to contemplate. Competitors have to push to reach the top, to be able to be measured by Kona. Which means relentless, gut-grinding electrolyte-filled days of finding how much you've got, how much you can give, how much you can take, until enough is ENOUGH.

After Western States Lew said "what's next?" Ironman became an idea. Swimming and cycling were weak spots in the beginning but he learned to embrace Triathlon for so many different reasons, and the beauty of it from Lew's point of view was that if you were hurt or sidelined temporarily on the conditioning road you could switch to one of the disciplines and still exercise. Triathletes celebrate the challenge and the possibilities and the obvious fitness levels they reach.

The heroes are celebrated as they cross the finish line. They have triumphed through the transitions, possible mechanical failure of the bike, whims of nature and whims of the body. They really are the Iron athletes who breathe the rarified air and understand being alive on a very specific level. In their skin. They are drinkers of the wind.

"Let's give it up for Lew," the announcer says at Kona. The audience cheers, and Lew gets the garland and the wrap. At press conferences he will get all the respect he deserves for being a warrior athlete. Lew exudes a cheery, effortless optimism and it's hard to know how much of it traces back to his early years. The generation of children born at the time of the Great Depression have sometimes been called "The Silent Generation."

The landmarks of Kona will forever be etched in Lew's heart, even though he has become a distinct landmark of his own after racing all around the world and the country. He is unique and unusual, a figure who is recognizable and that people look to for inspiration. Being a leader takes commitment and work.

Lew had a loving family who nurtured his genius and if they didn't hear him anywhere else they certainly heard it when he learned to make explosions in his home lab as a kid. From early on he evidently felt empowered to think for himself and act on it. He saw patterns in Nature, and in the Table of Elements in particular, and he could understand how pieces fit.

CHAPTER 5   A POWERFUL LOVE (MEET ME IN OCTOBER)

He has made all the pieces fit with his ideas about working out, health and vitality.

"You look at one hundred miles and you say, "No Way! But can you take one step? And another? Eventually you'll be there, mission accomplished." Born in 1930, Lew came into a well to do family and was Lewis Jr. until his beloved father's passing when he was a young adult. Family finances related to the Depression forced Lew to leave private school and go public in the fourth grade. In first grade his teacher was so impressed with his powers of observation and focus that she kept him after school to study him and eventually ended up writing a thesis paper about him. In his own words Lew felt he stood out because he was sensitive, shy and bright. It was his father who taught him how to cope with bullies by teaching Lew how to fight back and how to speak their language.

And so when Lew is halfway around the world he will find a way to speak a common language, because there is a universal understanding among world travelers. But as the Depression influenced the family's business Lew's transition into public school gave him an abrupt entrance into the tougher neighborhoods and it was here that he learned how fast he could run and how hard he could fight back... Perhaps it was also here that he developed a taste for diving into the deep end and knowing he could surface, and maybe be stronger for it. We don't find out who we are until we are tested.

Lew's personal reservoirs run deep. He says frequently that he likes to "use himself up." At ninety, he is an incredible example of a dynamic person, and then in subtext, a dynamic senior. He doesn't care for labels or feeling boxed in and sure doesn't like playing the senior card. It's difficult to say how many different character traits have carried Lew to the point he's at today, but he has a list of much loved sayings, which encapsulate a deep and far reaching philosophy about life.

Transitions can be difficult. In races and in life. If Lew had not done all the shorter marathons around the country, if he had not been one of the top endurance riders in the world, his first application to Kona would not have been a good idea, especially at 55, coming after the completion of the mind-bending and body challenging Western States One Hundred at the age of 54. Details make a big difference in a triathlon such as Kona. For example, you don't want to be dehydrated after the swim because it's guaranteed the bike section will suck the fluids right out. Lew built on cumulative conditioning, success, orientation and philosophy. At ninety, he still gives the impression that he's playing when he runs up a hill when other people his age are sitting in the old arm-chair or worse. His completion of so many Ironman competitions may have helped him morph into a really interesting man.

In 2012 at the age of 83, he became the oldest man to complete an Ironman Triathlon when he finished the Hawaii Ironman. Even though that record was subsequently broken Lew still holds the Guinness Book World Record for that Race. He finished the grueling competition in 16 hours, 45 minutes and 52 seconds. A testament to the Triathlete's Prayer that anything is possible and that you can make life the grandest experience, beyond your wildest dreams.

CHAPTER 6

IF YOU ONLY KNEW KONA, LIKE LEW KNOWS KONA

Lew did quite a bit of preparation to know Kona. As has been said, he does everything he can and studies what the needs are going to be for races. But Kona is like one of those wildly exotic, beautiful and exciting friends who will always short sheet you when you're not looking. And with Kona most would agree it's the winds that could short sheet you. Put there by the Gods of Triathlon to see how bad you really want it, because when force working against you is multiplied by how hard you're trying, it can be exhausting.

Because participation in any Triathlon takes many qualities including speed, endurance, a little luck and lots of training. And then there are all the intangible qualities like focus, determination, and the desire to complete.

Speed, endurance, luck and training. Start off the day with a 2.4 mile ocean swim of Kailua-Kona, and then transition without resting, not wanting to waste precious seconds. One hundred and twelve miles on one of the toughest bike courses in the world, specifically because of the wind and humidity, and then without wasting a second contemplate the marathon section of 26.2 miles.

Lore has it that Kona was started as a beer bet among 15 men. It is considered to be one of the world's most prestigious one day endurance events, and the people who enter it don't back away from a challenge. In 1998 Lew was entering his ninth Kona Ironman and he said his goal for the bucket list was to complete 10 Kona's before he couldn't do it anymore.

Imagine an Ironman training 18-24 hours a week for a race that maybe 90 degrees humidity with headwinds of 35 miles per hour.

It could be said that Lew started preparing indirectly for Kona in the mid-sixties when he started endurance riding, even though he'd always been an athlete. By the time he quit full time effort in that arena he was doing the really long endurance rides, the ones that went on for 150 miles. Riding a bike uses the same muscles as riding, and he always did like to run. But riding a triathlon bike is a horse of a different color and the training rides he went out on for awhile with the cycling group in the beginning were a training in humility. He got left behind a lot.

And the question that may have helped goad him into becoming an accomplished cyclist in triathlon was being asked about his equipment.

"What's a matter Lew, did you get a flat tire?"

Lew remarks that for Western States he did the longest training runs, practice runs for up to six hours in a day. The only reason that didn't seem like too much is because he'd been running marathons all around the country before that. If Western States is as beautiful as it is tough, what can you say about Kona? It will definitely rock you, even if you're just watching. That's how big the magnitude of it is.

It helps if you speak Ironman, because it's a specific language. You know ahead of time that Kona is one of the toughest Ironman races in the world, and that the weather and the course itself will strip down what you thought you had and leave you hanging on just to finish. Triathlon originally comes from Greek origin meaning three competitions. In the seventies, when jogging became like an antidote to civilization, America started its' own version of the three competitions in one, and Kona Hawaii became like the mother of all triathlons. No one wanted the top athletes to rest on their laurels for too long.

The second weekend in October, as it turns out, is sort of a perverse Christmas for elite athletes of triathlon because they get tested, and then they get tested some more, and then they come back the next year. For Lew the second weekend in October would go on for over two decades when he won international attention in his age group on a regular basis. He came into the first one at the age of 55 after completing Western States one year earlier.

He loves triathlon because of the variety of challenge and the ability to condition by swimming, running and cycling.

"Ocean water is salt water which gives you more buoyancy but in either fresh or salt water the trick is to find a draft off of a swimmer slightly faster than you and just stay on his or her feet," Lew explains. "So you get maybe 15% more efficiency saving energy that way. But you have to be quick or the person who can swim faster than you will be gone and you cannot catch them. So it is a game to get a good draft."

The 2.4 mile swim in the bay at Kona starts the morning off with swimmers backed in close to each other coping with swells and currents racing out to the buoy and back. It's suggested to swim in the bay beforehand to have some idea of how strong the currents can get. Every Ironman has different strengths. The hundred and twelve mile bike ride through lava country with powerful winds and demanding ascents and descents tests the best of the best. Much of the cycle segment is out on the Queen Ka'ahumanli highway(Queen K) with the goal being to make it to the point at Hawi before turning around and taking the descent where winds can blow you sideways if you haven't already been blown off going up.

Historically trade winds helped ships get between Europe and America. So visualize a ship being blown across the ocean and you get a small idea of what it can feel like to cyclists. In the Ironman Trade winds can sometimes make or break an individual's cycle portion if they knock the participants sideways or if the force is blowing against them the whole time. The heat averages between 82 and 95 but may post over one hundred degrees Fahrenheit.

Hawaii Ironman is viewed by many as "the ultimate showdown." Lew himself has said "It's horrible. It's the ugliest, toughest race ever." Why would you dance with something like that for 25 years? It makes for some great stories but it's probably one of the reasons Lew is still doing sprint triathlons at ninety.

What answer could you possibly be looking for in the Hawaii Ironman? Is there life after death? What are the bigger questions in life? Are there any answers? Or is it just pounding away everyday, chasing the Holy Grail, hoping you're not charging at windmills?

The more you exercise, the more the exercise feeds the brain. Lew has gotten some answers about the Hawaii Ironman but it's not certain he's shared them with the general public. His personal Odyssey in his incredible years of participating in the Hawaii Ironman can in some ways be compared to the travels of Odysseus. Good times, bad times, lulls, but no doubt heroic the whole way through.

There are plenty of rules in any triathlon. But in the Hawaii Ironman there's a lot to worry about. There are penalties if cyclists get too close together. Because of the force of the winds, it can be dangerous to take even one hand off of the handle bars to shift gears, take a drink or try to eat.

"For Kona the bike is the race," says Lew. "The wind is so strong it sucks everything out of you so for Kona I trained more on the bike. Get a good draft on the swim, tough it out on the bike, and run your best with what you have left," he advises.

Strategists may make up time coming down the Queen K if they can handle the acceleration. Hitting the wall, bonking, or getting in the zone and forgetting to get out can be problems. Lew has said frequently that his greatest thinking comes to him when he's running, but the test of the last 26.2 marathon miles after the Swim and the Cycling portions takes endurance and heart past the normal levels into something that's hard to comprehend unless you are the one doing it.

The Hawaii Ocean Science Natural Energy Laboratory is situated approximately halfway through the running segment of the marathon. It's said that sometimes runners in the line look like they're on a death march.

The Lab Site gets more solar radiation than any other place on the western continent. According to Google, the last few kilometers of Ironman have impaired the human body simply because of the sheer beating it's taken starting with the swim in Kailua Bay with the tropical fish, reefs and a horde of jammed up swimmers. By the time the bike section is done there has been serious effort.

Before the official Hawaii Ironman was put together the separate bike race that use to be run was hosted over two days, indicating the depth of the challenge with the elements and the activity. The Hawaii Ironman Triathlon was put together ultimately as a sort of test for the finest athletes to measure themselves. And they know they've been measured.

The muscles and the mind are drained. The stride length decreases. The Finish Line becomes even more important. First seeing it, then getting across it and finally an internal feeling of satisfaction mixed with exhaustion understood by the elite few. It's worth repeating that the Triathlete's Prayer is that anything is possible. If you want it bad enough.

At his home Lew has a room full of trophies, statues, belt buckles and ribbons. Each has significance. Some of the rewards are a little more intangible. Look at the comments fans make and you realize how respected and appreciated Lew has become by people who know him in the sports community. He's an inspirational dude. He absolutely rocks. People can't wait to share the course with him, whatever it is. Maybe they get that the way Lew races is a metaphor for a certain quality of life. 'I hope I am still doing this when I'm his age. I hope I can be as strong as you when I grow up.'

Kona of 2011 turned into a battle zone on a number of levels for Lew. He actually went into it with a hernia. In the swimming section he developed back pain which turned out to be the onset of a kidney stone. Then an old rival showed up to compete, illustrating the saying that rivalry makes the heart go stronger. Another saying, that senior athletes are unique and not antique. Lew has always embraced the elite competitive nature of

Kona. "It makes Kona special," he observes. But he remembers 2011 vividly.

After the swim and the relief of getting out of the water, Lew prepared for the cycle part of the race. The first section gives competitors false hope, because it's down hill. Then they hit the fishing village and the turn and the excruciating long hall to Havi, uphill, frequently with winds blowing against you and it's hot. "I couldn't take any nutrition," Lew observes. A careless hand off the handlebars with wind can cause severe repercussions at the speed they're racing. Not being able to put in sustenance worried Lew, but he said he just "Locked into finishing. It's all survival at that point," he observes.

When Lew started on the last segment of the race he actually had to hold his hernia at times. But he said that overall, he actually felt pretty good. And he won the distinguished award of being the oldest to complete the Ironman(at that time).

CHAPTER 7

PERSISTENCE

Lew wanted a different kind of a book on aging. As you read about his adventures and philosophies, you come to realize that Lew is a man with extraordinary spirit, a self-actualizer, and an athlete who understands what the human body is capable of with systematic training, conditioning, and an intelligent diet with supplementation.

Colonial Americans, Cowboys, Pioneers, all had to travel great distances the best way they could. By foot, by horse, carriage, trains, and wagon trains, never realizing that the age of relative ease was coming just around the corner with the possibility that it might take away as much as it appeared to give. Does modern civilization create an environment where mind, body and spirit are integrated, or does it sometimes do the opposite? For many endurance and health fell by the wayside when conveniences started creeping in. The quintessence of dust which is us at times seems to be replaced by an interminably long internet connection simulating real life. Lew has been chasing the goal of optimal physical health and vitality not only to be healthy and retard aging but to keep his brain functioning at the highest level possible. No doubt some of the co-working scientists who've made room for him in the lab would be surprised to see what he does in his spare time.

It's said that when will is guided by reason it's free, and no one doubts Lew's Iron Will though it maybe a bit of a cross for him to bear at times. In 2017 a PBS documentary showed Lew in a tough triathlon(Escape from Alcatraz) at the age of 87. The documentary explained how his increased activity keeps the red blood cells flowing across the thin surface of the lungs thereby carrying oxygen at high levels of efficiency to other organs and muscles of his body.

"If you do not challenge your body everyday it will follow the normal flow and slowly shut down and you die," he comments. "Pushing it goes with trying to extend my health into old age."

When he was 87 Lew had already completed the Escape from Alcatraz five times. None of the many documentaries on Lew have ever fully been able to explain his mind set because he's a true phenomena. It's hard to resist because he is a physicist but there's a lot of 'mind over matter.' In Greek the word soul translates into "to breathe." And goes on to talk about reason, character, feelings, consciousness, memory and qualities such as perception. Lew has dabbled in a few scientific aids to slow down his aging but by and by it's still boiled down to a few familiar themes which are not secret but definitely special.

Persistence, looking in the mirror to make sure you've done your best everyday, goal setting, and the whole drill about going anaerobic everyday. Persistence is a mental quality that has made Lew an internationally known senior athlete and illustrates his theory that ninety per cent of competition is a mental game.

"I always expect the best out of myself," he says. Racing, competing all over the world, would not have been possible for Lew if he did not have persistent determination. How he was raised and the time he grew up in certainly helped to shape him but then he took off and hardly ever looked back. Persistence means something when he says it. He's raced with a kidney stone coming on, with broken ribs, and a cracked pelvis, and it's not just the accolades that kept him going. It's a joke among some ultra athletes that you're never alone because you've got pain. But he has the persistent and dogged satisfaction of excelling and knowing that he has given one hundred per cent.

There's predictable imagery in Lew crossing the finish line. He maybe tired, he may not always be happy, but the act of attempting the impossible just one more time has given him a chance to defy the odds and put a singular stamp on his existence. He is watched by fans all over the world, and he has infused hope into the idea of aging with some grace, satisfaction and dignity.

Are athletes bigger, faster, stronger than they used to be? Research and statistics indicate this as a possibility. It's a brave new world for those who step into higher competition. Nutrition, sports sciences and strength training have upped the ante but humans are still stuck with genetics. With new technology and body type adaptation to individual sports there has been an "Imaginative Explosion" into the understanding of what the human is still capable of.

Lew's an Ironman, and it seems like a balancing act, a juggling act, and at times a death-defying high wire act.

Pushing it to what seems like extremes is systematic, according to Lew, and even as he's grown older his concessions to being ninety don't come across at all like surrender though there maybe a bit of good-natured resignation. It's still a victory dance because everything he did when he was younger helped get him to the ninety that he enjoys today. So, you stay away from open windows, don't walk in front of trucks, and eat healthy.

Just ask his old friend Kona where he was the unofficial mayor. Kona spawned his Ironman identity probably more than any other competition. You swim in rough water in such close proximity to other athletes you'd think the oxygen could get sucked out of the water.

Then there are the whims of nature in the long cycling segment and a 26-mile run to finish.

Lew learned many adaptation tricks in the swim segment of triathlon. But one of his funniest swimming stories occurred during the Escape from Alcatraz Triathlon in San Francisco, California. The swim in the bay is notoriously difficult for a number of reasons. There's a powerful current flowing out underneath the Golden Gate Bridge. Lew had done the race a few times already and had seen swimmers taking what appeared to be short cuts through the prescribed course. When Lew tried the short cut he got carried so far away with the current he almost missed the gates or signposts which were the way back into the race from the exit from the ferry near Alcatraz Island.

He was in a wet suit and he climbed a sea wall and flopped back into the water on the other side, covered with barnacles from climbing over the sea wall. "That's my dad," his son would explain to a friend watching. Lew remembers when he swam through a vast stretch of dying anchovies on the Pacific Coast in California. The smell was over powering and the distance wasn't short. He can't forget swimming through two miles of dense, stinging jellyfish in the North Sea of Denmark in Frederichia in 2001 in competition. "The jellyfish were so thick that day in the North Sea that it was like swimming in Jell-O," Lew recalled. "There were actually nurses lined up to help swimmers as they came out of the water, shaving off the stingers." Lew got stung in-between two fingers. Blue jellyfish, orange jellyfish, a perfect storm of stingers. So when you see a certificate that says "USA Triathlon recognizes that Lew Hollander has earned the distinction of Triathlon All American Honorable Mention," you know he earned it.

In his successful book on endurance riding he notes that his kids observed that he solved all of his problems with physics and running. But somewhere along the way he also learned to be a leader. His accomplishments in the ITU (International Triathlon Union) World Championships are the stuff legends are made of. He won gold at Sado Island, Japan in 1998 and again in Denmark in 2005. In addition Lew won gold in the ITU Olympic distance in Vancouver, Washington in 2008. These are just a sprinkling of his accomplishments.

CHAPTER 8

AND NOT BE DEFEATED

Lew has completed the Escape from Alcatraz triathlon six times. But his completion of the race at the age of 87 in 2017 is a truly stunning victory for more than one reason. This is a shorter triathlon than some but so grueling and potentially hazardous that competitors half his age think twice about entering. In his younger years Lew carved out a lot of hours in the Bay Area doing heavy duty, intense, scientific work. So when he comes back to do a race such as this one it's a different way to catch up on friendships.

The Escape from Alcatraz Triathlon is iconic for a number of reasons. Take the swim for example. It is considered to be one of the more difficult swims in elite Triathlon. Early in the morning contestants board the Hornblower Ferry and head towards a point off of Alcatraz Island, the infamous San Francisco land-mark which used to house dark criminals. If the swimmers are lucky the water temperature will be about 55 degrees and if they're unlucky it will be much colder.

There are a lot of practical questions that need to be asked in a competition like this, like are there sharks in the bay? According to the information packet it is acknowledged that there are sharks in the bay and other marine life such as seals and sea lions. It's stated that the sharks that live in the Bay are small and hang out at the bottom of the Bay. "These sharks have no interest in triathletes," it's said. Larger sharks live outside the Bay where the salt water is the right concentration. Large sharks do not like the brackish waters of San Francisco Bay. And there are helpers on the water if seals or sea lions get in the way. Forget about occasional wayward whales.

The curious reader may want to pause, as in other sections of the book, and ask what drives Lew to leave his comfort zone on such a regular basis. It is a question shrouded in mystery but you have to remember that part of the Triathlete's Prayer is to arrive at the end of the journey and say 'wow what a ride!' So back to the intensity of Escape From Alcatraz! Possibly 2,000 contestants on the Hornblower Ferry out on the bay near the rocks and Alcatraz, and they have to jump into the bay within six minutes or they get pushed off. The Hornblower can't just hang around because there's a western river that flows underneath the surface of the choppy waters. This westerly river forms an enormous amount of water exiting the Bay per second. We don't want to focus on sharks or the temperature of the water at times or even the leap off the boat. But the endorphins and the adrenaline are flowing.

The current will make even the strong swimmers consider negative possibilities. It's so powerful that there are suggested landmarks for the swimmers to focus on so they don't get carried out. And so it is with life that we are sometimes stuck in a strong river flowing west out to sea. If we can site the right landmarks and swim strong, if we can persist, we have a better chance of making it to shore and dry land to continue the race. The allowed time for the one-and-a-half mile swim is an hour. Swimmers swim south away from the pull of the tide. They pick locations and landmarks like the mouth of Aquatic Park and the two Fontana towers near Hyde Street Pier. Suggested time is ten minutes per site. Other spotting points include the 3 piers at Fort Mason and the Wave Rock Jetty, the Dome of the Palace of Fine Arts and the Red Roof of the St. Francis Yacht Club.

Lew's number in the 2017 race was 2404. He's used to being a senior athlete in most of his races, but in this race he did earn the distinction of being the oldest to complete in the 85-89 category. He was filmed by a BBC Film Network as part of a series highlighting health and health in senior athletes, specifically Lew. It's suggested that having targets in sports and in life maybe good for not only physical well being but for mental health as well. As Lew went about this Triathlon the camera crews were following him and so were the amazed bystanders.

All watching and wondering what his story is. The route around Escape From Alcatraz requires advanced skills. The one-and-a-half mile swim is grueling, not like doing laps in a pool. The eighteen-mile cycle segment requires high technical skills and covers a lot of steep hills. Then there's the eight-mile run to Baker Beach.

Escape from Alcatraz requires tremendous focus. "I like to compete, and I have great power of concentration," Lew observes. "I can focus attention on what's at hand." Consistent performances in triathlons all over the world have helped cement Lew's reputation. His accomplishments indicate what a tough competitive athlete he is but at the same time Lew always finds a way to look out for and encourage those around him. "I do treasure the idea of sunrise to sunset consistency which once again returns to persistence as well as survival in nature," he says.

When you see the guy who's not afraid to throw it down in the heat of competition it's surprising to be reminded that he's a physicist who specializes in material science, which includes various areas of science, engineering, elements of applied physics and chemistry as well as chemical, mechanical, civil and electrical engineering.

"When I was around 6 I asked my father why the lights went on when we pushed the switch," Lew recalls. "He told me electric charge went through the wires and there was a positive and a negative and the light was in the middle. I was fascinated with what went through these wires and I spent most of my scientific career trying to understand how it worked," he explains. As Lew matured the question about how light flowed because of the switch got transferred to bigger and bigger questions.

"...Well, there are conductors and insulators and then there were semi-conductors," he discovered. "While in the Navy, stationed at the Naval Radiological Defense Laboratory in San Francisco, NRDL, I worked on nuclear radiation effects and instrumentation.

"But I also pursued my passion of semiconductors long before their full potential was realized. So, I had a good start in a new field which of course opened the gate way to the chip and what followed. So, I was there when it all happened and hopefully played my part," he explains. "I, like the rest of the scientists in the semiconductor world, started a semiconductor company in Puerto Rico." Lew's company was called Integrated Transducers. "We made the best audio transducers, the pick-up arms of phonographs used by Motorola," he recalled.

Lew attended Case Western University. There are 17 Nobel Laureates associated with this school. He's also familiar with a saying from Adelphi University where he earned his BA in Physics by 1951. "Vita Sine Litteris Mors Est." Loosely translated, it means 'Life without learning is death. The truth shall set us free.'

Fans who have followed Lew's remarkable career and especially those who have competed with him remark that he appears to be the same person at the beginning of a race as at the end. But if the Lew of today could have a conversation with the boy who made the vow to be healthy and age well, it would be an interesting conversation. Lew kept the promise. And without meaning to, he has ended up being an inspiration and shedding some light on a difficult subject. Aging. And while he's done his best on the complicated dance with fate, Lew knows that his life has been full of many miracles. He looks for them everyday, and maybe that's why he sees them.

"My life has been full of miracles," he always says. "Like I was bike training hard on China Hat Road (Central Oregon), and a black shadow passed over me so vividly that I wanted to see what it was so I pulled over to the roadside. Before I had even unclipped I could see a sports car coming by going at least 100mph. I would have been a goner(if I had not pulled over)," he recalls.

But along with his Quest on Aging, Lew has always had an interest in the spiritual and the supernatural and the way science will interact with mankind in the future. "Everyone knows there is a lot more to the picture of life and forces driving each of us than we know or are capable of knowing," he states. "Now most people are brain-washed by their parental and societal upbringing so when stressed they revert in desperation to what they are taught. The books show this over and over and it is true. The big question is avoided however. Are these fables man-made or inspired by a higher system? So the question remains, and maybe that is good, a mystery with no hard data, just faith.

I personally know that there is, in my life, an interaction with a force, spirit, angel, or whatever ever you want to call it. God? I also do feel that all of the religions of the world are man made and they do NOT know anymore about this GOD than I do, or any other human, and we should include the animals and molecules as we are all part of a universe and should respect, love and try to understand it," Lew believes...

"So we have great hopes and aspirations for the future," Lew has observed. "History has not been kind to the human race so far. The driving forces of humanity...have served evolution well on sex and food. I mean these in their broadest context—Procreation and Nesting is evident in all species, from our transition from hunter-gatherer, to city-states, our history is replete with massive destruction, torture, and genocide, all with the goal of obtaining dominance. Maybe, just maybe, Artificial Intelligence(AI), will look at the big picture and direct us in a more peaceful and happy direction. And maybe that is why we are here and is the way it should be. You could say that the evolution of AI created by man will lead us to the biblical prediction of the "Second Coming" around 2035. At that point in time AI will have sufficient capability to be able to paint a picture of "The Real Universe" and interpret, for the first time, our role in this new awakening..."

CHAPTER 9

ACTION HEROES

It would seem that this is a new era of make-believe action heroes. But the Action heroes are not real. In real life there is just no way to create a quick, real, action figure. The real action heroes seem to pass under the radar of general scrutiny. Without the initial intention of it, Lew has become a kind of real action hero to interested fans and bystanders all around the world. "The body is an amazing instrument," he repeats over and over again. It still amazes him and it seems like he wants to remind other people as well. His no rust, no dust approach to conditioning and competing is the best proof that his philosophy works. That's not to say that he's waltzing through a la la land of "isn't this wonderful and maybe today I'll go out and do a few squats" type of mind set. He starts his day, every day, with a challenging combination of stretches and strengthening exercises and he believes so firmly in the importance of the routine that he literally won't put his pants on until he's done them. Push-ups, leg lifts, and other routine stretches to reduce injury while sustaining flexibility.

The word heart is a homonym. The heart as a noun is the amazing organ that keeps all the blood moving and keeps us alive. "Heart" as an adjective describes someone who tries extra hard, who avoids quitting. "The secret," Lew repeats patiently, "is that there is no secret, no magic Holy Grail or fountain of youth." After finishing the World Championship 70.3 Ironman race in Clearwater, Florida, Lew was in line checking out at the Sheraton Hotel when the young lady behind the desk said "look at this man, 80 years old, who just finished the Ironman race." A man in the line next to Lew looked at him and asked "what do you take?" Lew responded "do you want to spend a day with me?" The man looked him up and down and said "no."

A sub script question about Ironmen is how they feel pain. Do you get more endorphins the more you work out, or is there a limit? As 90 Lew still expects a lot out of himself. His mirror doesn't allow for a lot of excuses. "When I look in the mirror I just ask myself if I did the best I could do today," he says. "I had to do my best, I have to pick myself up, and I have to keep trying. Quitting is not an option. If there's a good reason for not doing something, then I won't do it, but if it's a matter of not trying hard enough then I have to try harder."

In picture after picture of Lew running across the finish line, he is proving his own saying. "Go Hard, Live Long." He has set out a new idea for what it can mean to age. He went from being a champion endurance rider to evolving into one of the great senior triathletes in the world. Charging across finish lines, slogging through choppy water, laboring up monster hills, is all in a day's work or training, depending on how you look at it.

CHAPTER 10

KNOCKED DOWN, GET BACK UP AND GO

Dr. Steve Jonas has written a book called "Triathloning for Ordinary Mortals." In addition, he is a long time columnist for USAT who has run 256 races over a 36-year period. When asked he described Lew "as the epitome of the athlete determined to do his best on any given day on any given course."

Lew has had many harrowing trips on the competitive trail, but perhaps one of his worst and most notable occurred in the year of Y2K, 2000, at the Ironman New Zealand. In 1997 he had competed in the World Triathlon Championship in Perth, Australia and placed fifth in his age group(65-70 years), and was the second American to finish.

"In 2000 I saw an easy qualification chance for Kona at the Ironman New Zealand," he recalls. "There was only one entry over 70 whom I knew I could beat so I went by myself to the race in Tapo, South of Hamilton on the North Island. At the last moment my nemesis showed up. I had a good swim in one hour and seventeen minutes and I had been out on the bike about eighty miles or so with a twenty-minute advantage over my rival who I knew could run faster than me, so I was really pushing it on the bike," Lew explained.

"I reached for a sports bar in my rear pocket and it sort of flipped up in the air. I thought I really do not need this but then at the last second 'yes, grab it' so I leaned to grab the falling sports bar and flipped over the handle of my bike breaking two ribs and my pelvis. The other competitor.... rode by and never stopped but took full advantage."

Lew came to and started putting his bike back together while someone called the ambulance.

The doctor who checked him told him he had not punctured his lungs. But the full extent of his injuries were not understood until he returned home to the USA. Here the story probably should read, and so of course, Lew quit the race, went to the airport, and returned home. But that's not how this story went.

"I got on my bike," Lew remembers, "and the doctor said 'where are you going?'" Lew's answer will amaze many who understand the severity of the situation. "I came thousands of miles and I am going to finish this race." Then he rode off. At this point many readers may pause and wonder about the competitive spirit. Anyone who competes understands this spirit, whether they carry it to extremes or not. It's the Fire and the Ice, and it's the warrior who goes back into the fray. Which Lew most definitely did. According to Lew he could ride to some degree in that position but getting to the transition "I could not get off the bike and I could not walk."

So here he is having one of the worst days of his competitive life and there are no friends or family around to help him simply because he could not have foreseen a difficulty of this magnitude or seriousness happening.

"...I got my transition bag in my teeth and crawled into the changing tent and put my shorts and shoes on. Well I can stand. I can walk slowly. So I started on the slowest marathon(run) of my life. I could not run, laugh, sneeze, etc, but I finished the marathon segment in seven plus hours. They put me on a stretcher and said they would take me to the hospital," he remembers. "So I laid there. Then I found out that the hospital would not do the x-ray until morning. There were national guard soldiers there who helped at the event. I called a young fellow and asked for help," Lew said.

He was helped to his car but then the nightmare continued. When he got to the hotel it was locked so he actually was crawling from door to door at about 2 a.m. in the morning.

"I was really lucky a person was near and they let me in so I crawled up the stairs to my room and got a shower," he said. "Next day I got a ride to a hotel in Auckland by the airport. I could not move for three days. When I finally got home to a doctor a nuclear scan showed the broken pelvis."

The doctor told Lew it would be six months before he could run or ride a bike again. "I need to be in Germany in four months to do the Ironman in Roth," Lew told the doctor. It was a promise to himself that he would not be defeated by the horrific ordeal he'd just endured. About four months later he was back at the airport.

"I limped as I got on the plane (to Roth). I did the race winning over several good competitors," Lew said. "I finished in thirteen hours and thirty-seven minutes(total) with a swim time of one hour and twenty minutes, a bike time of five hours and thirty one minutes, and a run time of five hours and thirty one minutes. I was seventy years old and I got my slot for Hawaii," Lew remembers. He had won the Roth, Germany Triathlon(in his age group) and the victory was especially sweet after so much trauma. He said the people on the streets in Roth cheered him on and even tried to push him up the hills on his bike, which was actually a little unsettling. But their spirit was genuine.

If you have completed this chapter you have a better idea of how the phrase Iron Lew really fits. You may wince as you have read this chapter, but you will probably never forget it.

"I am not anything special," Lew remarks. "I put my pants on one leg at a time just like everyone else. My DNA is not special, my background has a smattering of success and failures just like everyone else. Maybe, my only quality is persistence. I like to say it takes guts to get out of ruts. I can concentrate on a goal and persist until it is achieved. I am a scientist and I try to look at the whole picture. I look 2-40 years later."

The race of life is a big idea and Lew has grappled with how to do it the very best possible way. "Well, we will see if I can win that race of life," he observes. "We are all going to die. There are two things you have some control over." Lew sees it as quality of life and length of life. Lew believes that you have to work for the quality of life in your later years, and that will help influence your "termination date." As for Lew, he will do his best. "I always need to account to the mirror(which he equates with conscience). And the question always is, "did you do your best today?"

CHAPTER 11

THE GLORY ROAD

Tim Yount, Chief Sport Development Officer for USA Triathlon and 30 year Team USA Manager, recalls that he watched an interview before Lew's ninetieth birthday where Lew remarked to the interviewer that he ran up a hill behind his house everyday. Not only that, he's going anaerobic, which means he's pushing it until he's out of breath, pushing hard.

"It got me to thinking," Yount reflected. "Who does that? One conclusion is that Lew is as tenacious as our top athletes. Need I say, this is so consistent with the mindset of all of our top stars, almost like it's part of their DNA."

Training, discipline and diet have all played an enormous amount in Lew's success and endurance, but he will repeat over and over that it is basic persistence and consistency that have helped him achieve so much. His stretching and morning strength exercises begin the day, and many who force themselves to stretch and strengthen know that these routines not only help the body, they help the mind.

Hard work and determination apply in every day of life. "People with that drive can achieve all the goals that they set, regardless of ability," says Lew. Because he's a scientist, Lew has never taken aging or the accepted wisdom at face value. If you work hard you get results.

When you look at Lew, you don't necessarily see a ninety-year old senior. You see some one who's helping to redefine and clarify how aging can look when you're vital, healthy and interested. Looking after your body is an important part of looking after your brain. Lew believes that because of his cardio-vascular fitness he is keeping his brain supplied with the blood that it needs to keep functioning well. He believes that the anaerobic training that he still practices everyday forces blood into all the little blood vessels in the brain and keeps it working.

For a long time Lew kept all of his certificates, many pictures and other honors in a couple of big cardboard boxes. You could pull out certificates related to honors in the study of age. Such as Lewis E. Hollander, Jr. is an active member of A4M, a society of Physicians and Scientist dedicated to enhancing the quality and extending the length of the human lifespan. This organization, composed of the American Academy of Anti-Aging Medicine, the World Anti-Aging Academy of Medicine, the American Board of Anti-Aging Health Practitioners, and the American Board of Anti-Aging Medicine, is looking for a better tomorrow and Lew is living proof of the possibilities of pushing back the aging frontier.

Lew's diet doesn't allow for a lot of indiscretions. This is a rough take on his morning meal::

"My morning mix is mainly based on AIM* products which provide most of the nutrients needed daily plus a number of other things. I mix a ten day supply then take it daily. I use pomegranate and aloe juice," he says.

AIM Barley Life powder sprouts covers a lot of bases(1tbs)

AIM CalciAIM most useful form of calcium and magnesium(1 tsp)

AIM Redi Beets supplies nitric oxide essential for ATP cycle(1 tsp)

AIM Propeas(1tsp)

Lecithin Granules-it is solvent(1tsp)

L Argentine-an amino acid which also raises your nitric oxide levels(1tsp)

Mace powder reported to improve your sex life((1tsp)

Vitamin C(1tsp-about 5 grams)

Protein powder(Combat)one scoop

Then I also take B-12 subliminal(1tbs) and a mix of Glucosamine, chondroitin and MSM. Plus about 900 Mg of CO Q-10 plus the usual B complex, D-3, Vit E with Selenium, resveratrol, Vit E (be sure to get the complex not just alpha).

If you look at the comments on Lew's web pages they are a true testament to Lew in the kind of respect he has earned for all that he's poured into on his journey across the Glory Road. Lew wouldn't call his succession of races and accomplishments the Glory Road but most everyone else would. He gets free-floating admiration: "...Inspired as heck, Lew rocks it, such an inspiration... I hope I am still doing this when I'm his age... can't wait to see him cross the finish line... this guy's phenomenal, inspiration to many, can't wait to share the course with him."

What is great? If it's real you hear about it, notice it, try to learn from it and are glad that it's there. In an age of quick fixes and overnight sensations that flash in the pan but provide no leadership, Lew comes across as a refreshing alternative. Another comment you hear from people who have competed with Lew is that he's very encouraging, especially to the up and comers, no matter what the sport. He gives encouragement, insight, and additional drive to do what seems like improbable but proves possible. STEP UP THE GAME.

A partial list of statistics on races(see complete tables in back of book), read like something a visionary would suggest, not something a mere mortal has done. IN the evolutionary process Lew has shown that modern man can swim more, bike more, run more and ride more, if he/she will just begin to GO HARD so that he/she can LIVE LONG. A partial history of his marathon competitions would include the Devil's Lake to Lava Camp Marathon in August, 1995. In April, 1990, he competed in the Hells Canyon Run. He completed the Tucson Marathon in 1996 and 199. Ran the Las Vegas 5K, the Seattle Marathon in 1995, the Cal International Marathon in 1988, 1993 and 1979. Keep in mind that he was always keenly aware of past times and interested in smashing them whenever possible.

Portland is only a few hours away from Lew's home in Terrebonne,

Oregon and he ran the Portland Marathon in 1978, 1979, 1982, 1983, 1984, 1986, 1987, 1988, 1989, 1990, 1991, 1994 and 1996. These astonishing records are even more notable when considering that in the early years Lew was still extremely competitive in endurance riding.

He likes a saying by Benjamin Franklin— "By failing to prepare you are preparing to fail." So as he came to be known in the realm of the Ironmen and the Iron Gents it was clear that he had done a lot of road work to stay on the Glory Road. He'd become a warrior. Lew completed the San Francisco Marathon in 1980 in 4:22:19. He ran in the San Diego Marathon in 1999, 2000, 2001 and 2002, coming in second in 2002. All these races may appear now as foot notes to Kona, but they were singular and momentous and probably even fun in some cases. Because he was building the blocks, putting everything in play, for the larger stage.

In 1983 he ran the Boston Marathon, the New York Marathon in 1980 and 1983, the Montreal Marathon in 1981, the Skagit 50 mile ultra in 1982, the Western States 100 mile in 1984, the American River 50 miler in 1993 and the McKenzie River 50 miler also in 1993. Athletes are singular individuals and what might look like overloading for some obviously would not be for others, as long as the groundwork laid the right foundation.

CHAPTER 12

PERFORMANCE DRIVEN

If Lew has had idle moments they've been few and far between. He graduated from the Cheshire Academy in 1947 at the age of 16. He then attended Adelphi University, graduating with a BA in Physics at 20. Adelphi is Long Island's oldest university, and can boast of having such illustrious teaching staff as Harlan Fisk Stone, who went on to become a Supreme Chief Justice on the US Supreme Court. The motto of the school "Vita Sine Litteris Mors Est" translates loosely into "Life without Learning is Death. The Truth Shall Set Us Free." Driven to be a scientist, Lew set his sights on high goals as his career as a physicist brought him into the challenging areas of material science.

Lew graduated from the Cheshire Academy in 1947 at the age of 16. He then attended Adelphi University, graduating with a BA in Physics at 20.

Lew attended Case Western Reserve Grad School in Ohio. Case Western Reserve Grad School in Ohio invites students today to apply if their performance record has been outstanding. It's considered to be the top ranked private research University in Ohio and one of the best research Universities in the country with an outstanding engineering school. Students with a good record at Case will catch the interest of a lot of top companies.

He's listed in the Who's Who in Frontiers of Science and Technology 1985 2nd Edition, Who's Who in Science and Engineering 2000 5th Edition and Who's Who in the West 14th Edition 1978-1979.

"Science is a serious profession. It involves a long term view with planning and diligence, each experiment adds a little to the store of knowledge and that aids Progress," Lew observes.

There's a palpable kind of intelligence that Lew exhibits, a low-key intensity that complements the way he seems unassuming but actually looks quite distinguished. Make no mistake about it though he's got a dry sense of humor and an active curiosity, and apparently always has.

"I started at about six or seven making of course gun powder," he says about his early years. "In those days anyone even a six year old could buy potassium nitrate, sulfur and charcoal. I would put it in a sealed can and place a candle under it. Bang. I had it out in the garden one day waiting for it to blow and my father walked by. Should I tell him? Then he might curtail my experiments. Fortunately the candle blew out. I then learned about fuses and how to make them. Then I was in business. By ten maybe I developed a mixture based on potassium perchlorate, a highly oxidizing agent(this is what you want for explosives. It was used as a mouth-wash because it released oxygen which killed germs).

It was so good it blew up if you lit it or hit it....

I was so excited about my mixture that I actually sent the mixture to the War Department to help with the war with the Germans. My mix would go off with any spark or concussion. It was great.

To my surprise I received an answer and it said, "Dear Mr. Hollander, (well no one had ever called me Mr. Hollander before), thank-you for your mixture. However we would like to point out that we would like to detonate the explosive when we want to and be safe to transport and store before use.' Well, I had not thought about that," Lew recalled.

"Then there was the time later when I got better at explosives, I made some crystals that blew up as they dried and it was a hot night and they started blowing up like bang, bang, bang. I ran and dumped them down the drain with lots of water which was a bad idea," he commented. "They dried out in the sewer pipes and all I heard all night was that bang, bang, bang. I was scared that several would dry at the same time and blow the sewer pipes apart but my mother and father slept through the whole thing." Lew ended up making lots of little devices for himself and his friends.

"I had many explosives and made and sold them. I was in the arms business at ten. I did a lot of experiments in the basement, I have always had a lab of some sort. I eventually got to play with the atomic bomb and that was great. Not many folks have witnessed nuclear explosions at the test sights. My discoveries came from seeing a need and putting technologies together to accomplish or improve existing methods of doing things. I love science and chemistry. It is like building blocks. Each has a place if you can see the place you get results," Lew states.

By high school he was working full time during the summers from age 13 to age 16 at the New York Testing Lab in downtown New York City, which he says was an hour commute each way from where he lived. In college he worked for the Long Island Daily Press as a District Manager and he also had a job filling cigarette and candy machines full time in his last two years of college where he graduated at 20 with a BA in Physics.

After becoming a physicist and joining the Navy he was stationed at the San Francisco Naval Radiological Defense Lab for his entire tour of duty.

"I worked at test sites and made measurements at many atomic bomb tests," he says. "So the point is I really moved up to the big one."

After participating in so many bomb tests his response is not surprising. "...We would sure as ---- hate to see a bomb go off in a metropolitan area. I bet one over New York would kill 20-30 million and render the land uninhabitable. Before relocating from Santa Cruz, California, I studied the weather patterns all along the West coast. You do not want to be east and I found Central Oregon was one of the safest places to locate. We have had one test called Mt. St. Helens and more fall out landed in Newfoundland than Bend. So I moved here. Also note in case of attack take iodine (iodine 131 beta emitter thyroid cancer) and canned milk (strontium 90 replacement for calcium in the bones)."

The seriousness of his work cannot be underestimated, but he recalls one break he took in particular.

"I was coming back from a bomb test and laid over in Pearl Harbor at the BOQ, officer's quarters, for a few weeks of sun on the beach at Waikiki, and then I was walking to report in for transportation after my rest... in Hawaii when a black limousine pulled up and asked if 'I wanted a lift," Lew recalls.

"It was an admiral and he asked where I was going. I said to the Commandant of the 12th Naval district and he said I am the commandant of the 12th Naval district. I told him about the bomb and I was instantly very valuable to him as they knew nothing about nuclear warfare. He took me all through the building including lunch and to where I was to report. The chief looked at my orders and said 'Lieutenant where the hell have you been and I said 'my orders are top secret orders' and I did have the Admiral behind me so no worries."

Lew says he was born to be a scientist. Due to the way he has taken care of himself, he has spent about one per cent of his retirement income on health care... For example, in a Ride & Tie Newsletter there is a message about Lew. "It is fun to see the young ones coming up. Of course then there are guys like Lew Hollander who are going faster and never seem to age. For the rest of us mortals, time takes its' toll." Lew has been quoted as saying that when he was young he always wondered if old people could do two things: bend over and touch their toes and have sex. This achievement oriented yet pragmatic approach to life has allowed Lew to reap huge rewards. Competitive spirit has nothing to do with aging, says Lew, though you do lose some quickness, agility, range of motion and a reduction in maximal output.

For Lew battling time has turned into a kind of elaborate dance. "You have to push your body to its limits," he explains. "When you do you find you can really extend those limits."

Time can be defined as an indefinite, unlimited duration in which things are considered as happening in the past, present or future. Every moment that ever has been or will be.

Competitive athletes hear the seconds, minutes and hours clicking away and drive themselves harder to keep time with the clock. But when you're inside the zone, and the endorphins and the sweat and the sugar are all blending into some kind of happy homeostasis, the true believer may feel like they're coming inside time, for a brief suspension of time.

Being an athlete warrior Lew has done some deep thinking. One of the many favorite quotes that resonate with him came from Alexander the Great:"I want the best doctors to carry my coffin to demonstrate that in the face of death, even the best doctors in the world have no power to heal. I want the road to be covered with my treasure so that everybody sees that material wealth acquired on earth, stays on earth.

I want my hands to swing in the wind, so that people understand that we come into this world empty-handed and leave this world empty-handed, after the most precious treasure of all is exhausted, and that is TIME. TIME is our most precious treasure because it is limited. We can produce more wealth, but we cannot produce more time. When we give someone our time, we actually give a portion or our life that we will never take back. Our time is our life."

Our Time is Our Life. To use it wisely, so we don't lose it.

Lew says it's exciting to continue racing at his age.

"And that's what life's about," he concludes simply. And when the hours, minutes and seconds to the finish line lose their meaning because you are past exhaustion, then you pull out something that is not currently a popular pc word. "Heart." Lew admits that cutting down on the length of his races is a fact. He has alluded to the extreme triathlons in a joking way as "near death experiences." Living on the carefully constructed edge, because it's easier to fly from there. In Lew's opinion, everyone makes life and death decisions every day in regard to their health and he has optimized his health by eating right, taking plenty of vitamins and amino acids, and exercising. His advice to all is "to go anaerobic everyday....push a barrier."

PHOTO GALLERY

Record time for an Ironman race 70 +
12 H.r 58 Min. Florida 2000

12 58 Fastest Time for IM Over 70

Finisher 2002 Hawaii Ironman 14:43:40 at Age 72
with Grand Daughter, Chantelle Shields

*2004 Hawaii Ironman
Bike and Run*

Performance of the Year from Ironman World Championship Corp. 2010

Lew Hollander 80
15 Hours
48 Min 39 Sec

Course Record

Bike, Run – Lew at Hawaii Ironman Kona
in his Late 70s

Galveston TX
IM 2011 – Lew 81

Lew at 87

PDX Sprint Triathlon –
Lew 90 Years Old

Lew's Wall of Medals –
23 from Kona Hawaii
Note the Table
has 78 Belt Buckles

Lew at 90

Finishing the Western States 100 Mile Run from Squaw Valley to Auburn – 28 hours

Lew in Guiness World Records   New me in wet suit.

Lew and Ryan at Smith Rocks 2020 – 90 years old

LH Biking Santa Cruz 85 years

The Thinking
Athlete's
Sport
History,
Strategy and
Camaraderie
at the Ride
and Tie World
Championships

Ride and tie 2011 Lew was 81 with Dave Wagner

Ride and Tie with Partner Doug Madsen

Ride and Tie 2015 Lew is 85, the oldest ever to do the R&T World Championship finished 11th with Wash Blakley. Southern Oregon

Lew on Lucky – Mount Adams Ride and Tie

Lew in Dubai UAE
January 2016

Lew awards Dubai UAE
2015 85 years old

Lew in Bahrain 2015 IM Race 85 years

**Lew at 7
Feeding Ducks**

**Lew as a Naval Officer,
Korean War**

*Lew as a Scientist with an STM (Scanning
Tunneling Microscope) I Nano Lab in Arhus, DK*

PHOTO GALLERY

Lew – 87 Years Old with Karen
LH-KJ Balloon Ride 2017

Lew – 85 Years Old at Top of Mt. Tumalo, Oregon

Lew – 90 Years Old with Karen at Mt. Bachelor Zip Line

Mis P (the horse) Heather and Dad

CHAPTER 13

UNDER THE GLARE OF THE ELECTRONIC BLACK MOON

The Past, Present and Future of the world have given Lew plenty to ponder, especially because he's always said he gets his best thoughts when out running and he's done a lot of running. In this day and age, when there is so much virtual reality, who doesn't want to recreate the world?

Lew created several worlds in the fascinating science fiction novel "And Chocolate Shall Lead Us(based on an idea that people listen best when it sounds sweet)." This is a story "linked to a paralleled past and catching a foreboding glimpse of fate." Entertaining, enlightening, and a little dark, much like the future of the world actually does feel like at times. "And Chocolate Shall Lead Us" puts a lot on the table in a very short time, and in more than one universe, no less. It opens in Venus in a chapter called "Going to Hell."

The dying embers of a once great society smolder towards extinction under a dead planet's soil, telling a dark story of people who destroyed themselves. It is 190,786 of the Venusians calendar or approximately 100,000 BC in Earth chronology. A subterranean family who look like segmented worms with enormous heads live life in a tiny apartment and recreate the world as it once was through virtual reality. The male Jonic is a thermodynamicist who specializes in the nuclear cooling system that helps keep the community alive.

Their child Kylia was bred in a fetal farm. Jonic tries one day to explain to his child how it was "before the heat forced them into hell."

USE IT OR LOSE IT

Kylia reasons that adults talk about going to hell. Hell is a hot place and maybe you send yourself there. It looks like for this little community that hell is just where they are going. On his computer Kylia remembers looking up "the green house effect."

The novel jumps around in dimensions back to earth and a scientist named Josh Van Dever who is about to make a huge discovery. A signal of sufficient interest to the scientific community is coming from the Ross Ice Shelf of Antarctica. Here we need to interject that the cold light of analytical truth is what scientists get to deal with, and that in many ways "And Chocolate Shall Lead Us" probably addresses many themes getting kicked around in Lew's brain for awhile.

Lew has always been interested in science fiction, likes the writings of Ray Bradbury and is fascinated by the Kubrick classic 2001: A Space Odyssey. In his novel Lew touches base in many areas. For example the scientist, Lars, has worked on the Search for Extra Terrestrial Intelligence, or the SETI program, and has been assigned "to listen to space noise and look for intelligent life out there."

So when the shell is discovered in the depths of the Antarctic Ice it is dubbed The Messenger. After much analysis it's discovered that the shell is a computer.

"Interest is high, fear is reduced, knowledge is power." Fourth Chapter(Venus-The Trial).

Along the way it is revealed that the community of Venusians is governed by a collective. All "leaders must pass a rigorous system of testing, including brain scans and analysis, to find leaders who are selfless, loving, dedicated individuals...From childhood, everyone is retested, annually for leadership potential, physical fitness and achievement skills. And since those seriously lacking are considered for banishment, there is a great incentive to learn and become a serious part of a productive community. On the surface, leaders achieved their roles by family position, money and power."

It was those leaders whose greed caused this terrible situation...during the surface days, the primary decisions were made by leaders, mostly self-appointed and selected by power, corruption, and other negative influences.

"And Chocolate Shall Lead Us" is an imaginative science fiction novel which looks at the past, present and future of the world. Who Chocolate is and how the world can be saved shows that Lew has given a lot of thought to the deeper philosophies of mankind, what has influenced our history, and what hope there may still be for the future.

CHAPTER 14

EQUILIBRIUM

Moving forward, moving back, all those moments in the sun chasing down his destiny and wondering what it would feel like as he found it, realizing that it was the people and the places he's run, cycled, swam and galloped through that made it worthwhile. All that life!

What Lew seems to have found is that as he has embraced the world it has embraced him back.

Toughness drives that intangible quality called heart. Toughness and sound scientific principles applied to a disciplined training program. One of the key tenets of Lew's training philosophy is his most well known one, going anaerobic everyday. "A lot of people haven't gone anaerobic since they were fifteen," he jokes, but he's really serious about pushing it every single day to ask the body to renew itself. That's the Fountain of Youth. But he would stress again that anyone who has not been exercising would want to consult an expert before beginning any kind of regimen.

In addition to his disciplined regime of vitamins, supplements and diet Lew pushes past his aerobic barrier everyday. This discipline has enabled him to pull out an extra gear when he needs it that many people don't even know they have. When you feel the burn, you get the love from your body loving you back.

Lew's philosophies have helped him stick with rigorous training. His collection of sayings are from people in history and then some that he's tweaked himself.

"Knowledge is a shaft of light, like an arrow piercing the darkness of ignorance." If you ever get a chance to meet Lew his athletic and scientific credentials precede him by about a mile but one of the most interesting characteristics is that he's so down to earth. Another words, humble.

"I never was the fastest," he laughs. But for awhile now he's been one of the oldest competitors still competing, which is still the biggest prize, particularly when he's in better shape now at 90 than some people half his age. "I'm still alive," he smiles.

So you can look at his Guinness Book World Record Certificate and say "wow!" That's all you need to say. At that time, Lew was the oldest person to complete the Hawaii Ironman at 82 years, 129 days when he ran the 2012 Ironman World Championship in Kailua-Kona, Hawaii USA on 13 October 2012. All records are invitations to be broken, and this one subsequently was, but the honor for Lew still remains because he knows that race. It was also in 2012 that Lew broke the record that he set in 2011 at Kona. He finished the 2.4 miles swim, 112 mile bike ride and 26.2 mile run in 16 hours, 45 minutes and 52 seconds. It was his 23rd World Championship and he got to the finish line 3 seconds faster than the mark he had posted a year ago. That's inside time, that's marching to your own drummer, and that, as they like to say, is incredible.

What's just as incredible are the times he's posted all the way through his incredible "residence" at the Ford Ironman in Kona. For example, on October 13, 2007 he finished the Ironman in a time of fifteen hours, 46 minutes and thirty six seconds. Anything is Possible!! That's the mantra that many Triathletes aim to follow at whatever level they're at, and it's both a promise and a goal. Lew has literally blazed his Triathlon Trail all around the country, the continent and the world. He competed in the Canadian Triathlon four times and came in second three times. He raced there in 1992, 1993, 1997 and 2003. He competed in the Arizona Ironman four times and came in first twice. He raced there in 2005, 2006, 2007 and 2008.

He started competing at Kona in 1985, one year after completing

Western States and realizing that in a sense he'd been reborn, recognizing that limitation was just a word.

He raced there in 1989, 1990, 1991, 1992, 1994, 1995, 1996, 1998, 1999, 2000, 2001, 2002, 2003, 2004, 2005, 2006, 2007, 2008, 2009, 2010, 2011, 2012, 2014 and 2015 but was not able to finish that year due to really strong winds.

A month after he turned ninety, in July of 2020, Lew was selected by Why Racing(Pacific Northwest), to be their cover for Triathlete of the month. Everyone knows Lew at Why Racing.

"I am a physicist, triathlete, author, married to Karen," he explains. "We live adjacent to Smith Rocks Park, in Terrebonne, Oregon. I have done over 70 Ironman races including 25 at Kona. I finished Hawaii at 80 in 15 hours and 48 minutes. I finished Florida at 70 in 12 hours and 58 minutes. I finished Florida also at 84 years old. I qualified for Kona at 85, finished the swim and the bike ok but I could not run fast enough to make the 16:50 time limit. So what is Lew going to do after Ironman?

Three weeks later(after the last Kona), I get a call from "Suzie" claiming to be calling on behalf of his Royal Highness Sheik Nasser of Bahrain. I said 'of course you are' and was about to hang up. She said "His Highness wants to invite me to come to Bahrain in December and do the 70.3 Ironman.

"So I had a magic carpet ride, Emirates Air, and Royal court car for 10 days and the race day I was driven past all the athletes carrying wet suits, bikes and the usual stuff, past the parking lots to the transition area. They ask my number and then drove me to my slot. This is service," Lew observes. The subtext of this trip was to show people in that part of the world what senior athletes are capable of accomplishing with the right mind set and training, Lew explained.

"I finished that race and three weeks later Suzie calls again to say his Royal Highness wants to invite you back to do the half Iron Man in Dubai, UAE. I asked 'same deal?' and she said 'yes.' So I went back and did the race. At 87 the BBC came from London to film me which included the Escape from Alcatraz Triathlon. That was my sixth time at that race. As far as local races I have done the Pacific Crest 18 times… But the last three years have been the best and happiest years of my life thanks to meeting and marrying Karen. I believe my best years are still ahead."

Lew is known as a person who keeps things in balance.

CHAPTER 15

STRONG

Lew sees his life as being full of miracles. After experiencing so much in his life with family and friends and competition and training, he knows he's been blessed. The hard work and good timing didn't hurt. At around ten he already knew he wanted to age well and that science was the place to be. He was already selling and inventing, trying to do his best everyday. If you read his story there are a lot of memorable images.

Lew's mother was an Irish Catholic named Alice but her nickname was "Queeny." "Mother was a certified National Horticulture Judge," Lew recalls. "She would travel all over Long Island judging, teaching and showing at Flower shows. I would help and even exhibit. (At home)I had my own garden and a secret place under the front bushes where I could play with cars, tanks and castles."

Peg, or Margret Louise Hollander, Lew's sister, was born eight years before Lew. "My dad was a great athlete and good business man," Lew recalls. "I remember his friends called him "Lew" and I always thought that was cool. They called me "Lewis." When he died I became Lew. I think of him often." The spirit and passion with which Lew was raised seemed to have served him well.

However, in his own personal life sports has obviously been a dominant passion. He has stayed with it, going hard, always using it so that his health is a renewable commodity. He believes his life is full of miracles and serendipitous occasions.

Have Lew's last forty years been more remarkable than his first fifty?

With the right determination a lot is possible. Old age is replete with clichés, euphemisms and repetitive old problems. You can end up feeling like you are marooned on an island while the mainland is getting further and further away. Lew started planning for old age as a kid. He didn't want to be like some people he saw who were losing IT at thirty.

His perspective now is that you better have solid condition and health by 40 because it will be difficult to change it after that. He's convinced that if you don't have the track down by 40 at 80 you will wish you had and of course it will be too late. Lew says he's never been as fast as some but persistence is one of his most important qualities. So many of the people who used to pass him are not running at all now and he still is and he says he "feels great." Fast time, slow time, was it Einstein who said time was relative? If so, to who and what? As a matter of fact Lew found out recently that he has the knees of a teenager. He knows this because he hurt a knee and had to get it checked out. His knees are good. This brings us to a side topic. How do Ironmen feel pain? You have to assume that Lew generates scads of endorphins because he never quits moving. The truths he's learned are the truths he values.

He doesn't see ninety as an ending but a different kind of beginning. Change is constant. Where did Lew's drive begin? One saying from the Depression era was "use it up, wear it out, make do or do without." He suffered severe loss at around 18 but his family gave him a strong foundation so that he could start tapping into his foundation early on. They knew he was doing that when they heard his periodic explosions.

Lew's Theorems: About fifteen years before Lew was born Einstein published the special theory of relativity which becomes oddly pertinent to Lew as he began to establish his own theorem about aging. The theory of relativity encompasses many aspects but includes the idea that the rate at which time passes depends on your frame of reference. Lew decided early on to establish his own guidelines for aging. Use It or Lose It. Einstein's theory suggests that the faster the clock moves the slower time passes to someone in a different frame of reference. While Lew knows he is not ageless he is known for giving time a run for the money.

E=mc2 can suggest that energy and mass are interchangeable and they are different forms of the same thing. Lew's philosophy Go Hard-Live Long suggests you can push barriers of time if you go hard enough. Einstein's work suggested that gravity is a curve or warping of space. The more massive an object the more it warps the space around it.

To some aging is a kind of negative gravity that pulls us all down and makes us feel that we're in a poorly directed science fiction movie. Look in the mirror, feel like sitting down. Lew's theorem "get out of the chair" suggests that if you move your molecules so they don't rust you have a better chance of creating your own gravity field for aging...

Lew's Bedtime Stories For The Adventuresome: "So thirty years ago we were on a cruise and met a delightful couple," Lew recalls. He was J, the chief federal judge of a district in Florida. "He invited me to visit him at the Federal court house so I went. It was super security. I finally got parked and escorted to his top floor office. Then he took me to each of the courts, I think there were eight. He just walked in, and went right up to the judge, stopped the entire proceedings and introduced me to the presiding judge." They visited other judges, had lunch, and afterwards Lew got to see what was on the roof where there were military and aircraft in placement and air force personnel. He was told they were trying a big cartel drug dealer who had an army bigger than most small countries. Moral of the story: You never know whom you're going to run into so it pays to run fast.

While Lew became known as the unofficial mayor of Kona for his running and other athletic skills he had built them over a period of decades and had collected so many interesting stories that it's hard to choose. But here are a few:

"I qualified and entered for the Boston Marathon," Lew recalls, "but did not plan on going so I ran a 10K at COCC on Saturday but Boston is always on a Monday so not a good idea to run hard a few days before.

About halfway through the 10K race I was feeling good and said to myself "I am going to Boston." After I finished I went right to the Bend Travel Agent and got a first class ticket out that night and a hotel room close to the race. I bought a new pair of running shoes, a new suitcase, went home, threw a few clothes into the suitcase and off to the airport," he recalled. Moral of the story: Not everything is set in stone

Lew did the New York City Marathon twice. In 1980 he completed it in 3:52. In 1983 he ran it in 3:17 with an eye towards shaving it down. One of those years it was raining and storming hard, he recalls.

"The race starts at Fort Schuyler, I think on Staten Island, and goes on the Verrazano Bridge to Brooklyn, then the 59th street Bridge to New York up to the Bronx and back to Central Park. One year with the big rain in the huge tent with the mayor it all blew down. I found a set of stairs down to the boiler room for one of the forts buildings and someone grabbed me and said 'you're the last.' We were standing on the landing of the stairs…and I got talking to my best friend from grade school who had lived a block away from me. OK so the race is ready to start and we are on the bridge. Two miles long with the wind blowing hard and you can imagine what 20,000 black garbage bags look like that were handed out to the runners to keep them warm. In the wind they curl down around your legs and ankles. It was dangerous. Now with all the runner's energy put into the bridge it goes into simple harmonic motion, a low-key frequency vibration, a sway. I thought I was sick or dizzy and was sure glad to get off the bridge." Moral of the story: It pays to hang on tight when it gets tough. It takes power to thrive and excel when the going gets challenging.

Kindness Pays Off—A Miracle Story: "About 1960 I was a senior scientist at Lockheed, Palo Alto(California), living on a hill not far from an executive at HP," Lew remembers. "My horse Puck had gotten into my hay stack and I was trying to lead him out. There was a single electric wire which I turned off protecting the hay. I stepped on the wire to keep it down so I could lead Puck out being too lazy to remove the wire. I sort of stretched to move the horse while still having one foot on the wire which was heavy gauge I acquired from somewhere.

"My foot slipped off the wire and startled the horse which quickly turned around winding the wire around me and his hind legs so we both went down with the wire cutting into his legs and my legs and his rear legs planted solidly on my stomach. So I reached up and stroked his nose for twenty minutes or so before my wife could get a wire cutter and untangle us. I really learned to love that horse," Lew observed. "A horse's first instinct is to kick out but he just lay there with me all wrapped up together." Moral of the story-Expect a Miracle.

Lew has always been fascinated by how and why materials change, how they can interact with other materials, and what will happen when stress or forces is exerted on them. He recalls being in Waco, Texas and stuck his head into a laboratory at Baylor University where a group was hard at work.

"We know you," they all chimed in. Morale of the story: When you do great work, everybody knows you.

Basic counts when you are in a crunch: Lew recalls that he was out about fifty miles into the Western States 100 mile foot race. He was hot, dry and lonely.

"I had a peanut butter and jelly sandwich in my belt bag and was looking forward to it so I took it out. The sandwich was dirty, full of sweat, and disgusting so I threw it away but then said to myself 'Lew you are a scientist, you need the calories....Now this is a true story. I had not run more than a mile and there in the middle of the trail was a brand new, fresh peanut butter jelly sandwich in a clean zip lock bag," he says. "I ate it, and looked up and said 'thank-you' and kept going." Moral of the story: Basics are important.

Stretching is Important: To be flexible in your body prevents injuries and helps with overall health. Lew's routine, every morning, is to stretch and do strengthening exercises, literally before he does anything else. But in the body stretching perhaps it also teaches the mind to be more flexible and open.

Moral of the story: There's more than one reason to keep stretching.

All Tires Blow, Sooner or Later: Lew was participating in the Half-Ironman World Championships in Las Vegas, Nevada. "I am leading in my age group but not by much," he recalls. The 56-mile bike course out to Lake Mead and back to Las Vegas was fairly uneventful until about 15 miles to the transition to the run. "Bang, my front tire blew," he explained. "No worries, I have to fix it, can just screw it on and re-inflate tire with sealer in it. Oh dear, there is white foam everywhere except in the tire," Lew remembers. "I am screwed," he thinks. But just then, an angel appeared, like in the movies, except it was riding a motor bike, says Lew. The "angel" switched the defective wheel for a new wheel, told Lew he could pick up his old wheel at the transition, and helped him onto his bike and pushed him off "just like they do in the Tour de France."

Moral of the Story: Expect an Angel.

Work Is Rewarding:

The world has gotten to know Lew as a singular athlete but his experiences as a scientist and physicist have been challenging on a level that probably needs some appreciation as well: "I discovered the crystals, which are CdS, Cadmium Sulfide, while I was in the Navy at the Naval Lab. I developed a method to grow them and more important a method to attach wires to them with ultrasonic soldering. I did that all on my own—it was not part of my job but my boss was very helpful and encouraging in all my research efforts," Lew recalls. Moral of the Story-You always surprise people when you do more than is asked and sometimes there's a reward you weren't expecting.

But there's no denying Lew has lived an intense life as a scientist. "I was present at many atomic bomb tests and did bomb effect measurements," he explains. "It was interesting to see a whole city built in the desert—tanks, buildings, aircraft and about anything else you can imagine all around the bomb site. As I recall one such tower shot, I flew into ground zero 30 minutes after the blast to retrieve my samples." They always shot at dawn, according to Lew. There had been a whole city assembled the night before and the next morning there was only a big mound of black sand. "NOTHING," he recalls emphatically. "You need to see it to believe it and I promise you, you never want to see one. I was in a trench with special glasses. You see and feel the flash. Then you see the ground wave coming across the desert. Then it hits the trench and you see one side a foot or more higher than the other." Moral of the story—It takes guts to be a scientist.

CHAPTER 16

WAREHOUSING

It's a difficult subject for most people to contemplate. Whole industries have spun out the idea that they will take care of the older generation. Seniors will be welcomed with open arms for however long they last. The fact that they are there and not somewhere else may be hard to accept and possibly speed up other situations.

"I don't want to be warehoused," Lew says flatly. "You have to prepare for old age," he says. "It doesn't happen well if there's not a plan." Lew was on the Board of Directors of Oregon Exercise and Physiology and the Board of Directors of AGE University of Nebraska. Lew has followed a plan and it's worked. On top of that he never plans on retiring fully. He has published several books, has a publishing company called Green Mansions, and has written for more than 100 publications. He owns more than twenty patents, many of which are so highly specific you'd need someone to translate them into English for the lay-person. He's listed in Who's Who in Science and Engineering 2000, 5th Edition, and Who's Who in the Frontiers of Science and Technology 1985 2nd edition, and Who's Who in the West, 14th Edition, 1978-79.

Homeostasis is a process by which the body regulates itself and keeps normal functioning within boundary lines. As you age keeping the normal functioning within the boundary lines grows more challenging. Like one of Lew's favorites, "if you don't use the rudder you hit the rocks." But in the best of all possible worlds it seems that Lew has a vision that he'd really like to share. Doesn't everybody want quality if the life span is extended?

So start early, set sensible goals for health and then stick to it. Realize that the body is a miraculous instrument when played with some thought and consistency. To be as successful as he is Lew has had to be tough. His conditioning plan made him successful and set up a smoother track for growing older. For so many reasons he has become a cultural icon.

CHAPTER 17

THE WIZARD OF KNOW AND GO

If you spend even the slightest time around Lew you realize he's to the point and has a collection of sayings which back up philosophies that illustrate his points with very little explaining. The shorthand seems to be that if you don't get a lot of the sayings you might not get it when he really opens up. His words mean results.

There doesn't seem to be general agreement at what age an athlete becomes an aging athlete though 65 is common and 50, 55 and 60 come in chronological order. But an athlete with integrity uses the sport for good trying to keep the good and bad in perspective for the overall bigger picture.

Lew's sayings have a way of striking home. Like you only are really old when you quit playing and lose the ability to dream. Age is not all a state of mind but Lew is one of those seniors who has proven that a positive mind set helps you do the dance with aging and inspire those around you to do the same.

The taking of old age 1-2-3. Is it true that society perceives people with grey hair as getting ready to be passive? Not necessarily, but maybe, just a little. Passion, dedication and drive have carried Lew a long way. If you look at the picture of him crossing the Western States Finish Line at 54 after completing the one hundred mile run he looks happy and maybe even a little surprised.

"It's just so unbelievable when you learn that your body has actual capabilities you just have no concept of," he says. Until, of course, you push it to find out. Then everyday can be like a never-ending adventure.

But there's no doubt about it. Life is the ultimate endurance test. One of Lew's sayings from endurance riding is 'to finish is to win.' It embodied a whole philosophy about winning, about doing it the best way and for the right reasons and about being educated. And also, of course, to finish.

The competitive spirit--What happens to it after thousands of miles of racing in ball grinding adversity? You get pure essence without a lot of syrupy saccharine thrown it to the recipe. Lew is Jewish/Irish with a few other nationalities thrown in. In Lew's words his dad was always understanding, and helpful, and it made growing up a lot easier.

"When I was fourth grade in public schools(depression results), they had gangs, sort of, not to the extent that we have now, no drugs or guns, but you got beat up a lot," Lew recalls. "I was smart, shy and not very assertive. Perfect target. So my dad read this scene and hired the school coach to teach me boxing and also paid for Alfred(a nice kid from the other side of town and member of the desert rats gang), to train with me. Well we learned to fight and we became great friends and I was always welcome at any encounter with the desert rats."

He was born in 1930 onto the heels of change, or the wheels, depending on how you look at it.

"In 1939 I was nine years old and I went door to door collecting clothes for the poor, frozen, Finnish children because Finland had been invaded by the Russians. They were outnumbered a hundred to one and holding their own. I was moved by their courage and fortitude. Well a few years later the USA decided to be allies with the Russians against the Germans and the Finns became our enemies."

Running and philosophy have been intertwined through Lew's life. "Ever thought about who you really are and how you can find out? There is only one entity that knows and that is your inner self....Well I try to meditate and connect with my inner self. I have had good luck doing this and I call it "Inner Lew," he says.

The times when the truth flashes at you in this state are valuable to Lew. One image is that there is a large, beautiful, blue egg, room size, with beautiful gold trim like a big Easter egg liked we used to have with a window, Lew explains. The inside is lined with pink satin pillows and it feels very safe and beautiful. And I'm there, about 7 or 8, looking at the world in wonder with blond curly hair and an expression of amazement. Lew remembers this image of himself as a little boy in the safest, most beautiful environment--happy, comfortable, warm and loved.

"Well, you know, that is exactly how I feel inside. I am, I hate to admit it, a very little boy looking in complete amazement at the magnificent world around me. How it works, the blue birds, the flowers, the chemicals and how they react to each other forming our material world. I am more concerned about how and why things work and the function than the people. They are merely reacting to the forces of our environment, self-preservation and self-adoration.

CHAPTER 18

THE "EASY" CHAIR VERSUS THE POSSIBLE TRUTH

It's 2015 and Lew is at a press conference in Kona. His number for the race is 8205. He is 85. "There are not a lot of sports where guys my age can still compete," he recognizes. Lew was not talking in a theoretical manner having just finished the World Ride and Tie Championships a few weeks earlier and placed fourteenth. According to some experts endurance events do favor senior athletes because it's all a test of grit, mental attitude and fortitude as opposed to certain kinds of sports that test only speed or strength. Good nutrition, correct training, good genetics can all help slow down the "age of decline."

Do we start to lose muscle mass after the age of 30 which can lead to an overall loss of strength and power? Use it or lose it. BUT SOME SLIDE IN POWER IS DUE TO DISUSE RATHER THAN AGING ITSELF. Fear, passivity and perhaps misinformation could be contributing to the disuse. Most of the easy chairs around the world could be thrown into the woodpile metaphorically because it is apparently not the best place for seniors to hit the reboot button. Sitting in the chair.

The buff road warriors are the athletes who refuse to go to sleep in the snow, who have refused to keep pushing even if it takes longer to get there. High caloric intake may not be as necessary. Longer recovery time between hard work-outs is predictable.

Lew is a worldwide symbol and inspiration to those who follow his trail and who want to believe that as they get older they can continue to move it on out.

The Triathlete's Prayer covers a lot of territory. "Anything is Possible."

CHAPTER 19

THE VOICE OF EXPERIENCE

Lew has painted on a broad canvas and experienced elation from the joy of living large. There is not one inch of his five foot six approximately 160 pound frame that has not experienced full living. YOU FIND OUT WHO YOU ARE WHEN YOU ARE TESTED. Lew takes the forward dynamic to fast forward all the time.

Lew's life is like a montage slide show which is a testament to a life fully lived. He's always had drive and discipline combined with a "no bubble wrap philosophy." People who know him remark that he gives off a lot of encouragement. When he was little it seems he was fascinated with what made electricity flow through circuits and turn it into light. In a larger sense it seems he's always looked for the universal connection that will make things light up.

Lew's band of brothers and sister, the ones he's run and ridden with, seem to be joined by some invisible cord of experience. Almost like they're always reaching the crest of the next hill, waiting to see what the view will be. It's not the fountain of youth he's been experiencing, it's the fountain of sweat. His journey of self-knowledge includes love lost and found, six children, count less accomplishments in the scientific community, the ultra endurance community, the literary community and the arrival at a special place called wisdom.

He has successfully illustrated the "wow what a journey" credo. He's always been going, and arriving, it seems like everywhere. But the biggest journeys sometimes occur on the inside and they're private. It is certainly true, however, that Lew has also been at most of the racing events in Central Oregon, whether it was the high-powered Pole/Peddle/Paddle or some lower profile charity event for a good cause.

"Lew was my partner for Pole/Peddle/Paddle for many years and we always did well in the pairs category," recalls long-time friend Roger Daniels.

A familiar figure, just like the mountains, rivers and plains he's crossed back and forth, over and over again. One of his gifts is the effortless ease with which he inspires those around him to think they can do it to, whatever it is. Just Do It.

CHAPTER 20

THE SOUND AND THE MOTION

"It's not about how hard you hit. It's about how hard you can get hit and keep going." -- attributed to a lot of people.

For Lew there's been the sound and the motion, and to paraphrase a great author, it signifies everything. Applause and cheers. Internal Lew driving him on. Conditioning and training take over when red lights come on saying it's time to stop. Kona, Germany, San Francisco, New Zealand, Oregon, The Sierras, Washington, California, New York, Boston. The Mid-East, Florida, Nebraska, Japan, Norway and Santa Cruz. The list is amazing and it goes on. His natural curiosity has led him everywhere.

Performance of the Year, Performance of the Decade, cumulative performance on so many different levels, it's difficult to measure, and as a physicist he's made a career out of measuring the really small difficult things and the dangerous things. His athletic career has been so huge that even people who know him are hard-pressed to describe his unique phenomena.

People like Tim Yount(USA Triathlon 30 year Team USA Manager and Chief Sport Development Officer), will say that tenacity is the mark of most of the great athletes, which actually goes along with Lew's observation that persistence is key. "I'm an ordinary person," he's said many times. "I put my pants legs on one leg at a time. But I don't quit." As has been frequently observed, endurance riding gave Lew what could be called a solid foundation.

"There are two principles I have learned," says Lew. "The first is from the great philosopher Brer Rabbit, as envisioned by Walt Disney in The Song of The South. You have to make do with what you have got because that is what pays off in the end." This philosophy is so simple that most of us don't think about it, but it is the key to success in long distance events. After all, you only have what you have got, so that's all you can do. In doing, you will find out that's a whole lot, and if you use it, you will succeed. The second principle is one step at a time, one after the other. You look at 100 miles and you say, "No Way! But can you take one step? And another? Eventually you'll be there, mission accomplished."

With over a decade of competitive endurance riding and ride and tie competitions, giving me over 10,000 miles of completions and over 100 wins and best condition awards, I learned the above truths," says Lew. Endurance taught him how to accomplish what seemed like unobtainable goals, he explains in an excerpt from Endurance Riding From Beginning to Winning. "...It prepares us for other activities in life. For me, a dream was born when I rode the Western States 100 mile ride, The Tevis Cup, from Squaw Valley to Auburn, California in 1974. I had the privilege of riding many miles with Gordy Ainsley as he ran it on foot—the first to attempt and to succeed what seemed to all an impossible feat. Thus, the Western States 100 mile run was born and now it is the most prestigious ultra run in the world."

Everyone trains differently, for different races. Lew is known as someone who prepares and tries to figure out what the race will call for. In 1999 he ran the Millennium One Half Marathon in Las Vegas in one hour and fifty one minutes. In 1994 he ran the Copenhagen 15K marathon in one hour and nearly 16 minutes. He finished the San Diguieto one half marathon from 2001 to 2004 in a finish time of close to six hours. In a cross section of his races we see that in 1995 he romped through the Salem Governor's Cup One Half Marathon in one hour and fifty minutes. He completed the Dirty Half in the desert in 2004, 2005, and 2009. It took him only two hours and 42 seconds in 2004 to complete the San Diego Half Marathon. He averaged five miles an hour in the arduous McKenzie River Fifty Miler in 1993.

In short, if you had a multi-colored box of pins and a flat map of the world, and you put a pin in for all of Lew's races including how many times he did them, the world would light up like an uneven Christmas tree. It cuts across politics. It's just good old-fashioned racing for fun and competition with the end result of being healthier and feeling more in control of your life.

Take responsibility for health and be your own best friend. You don't have to race around the world to do that. Lew has flown around the world, repeatedly, representing the US, himself, and more recently, the hopes of seniors. He's given people who want to know a picture of what the world could look like if maybe the priorities were a little different. With his natural ability, his dedication, and the fire in his belly, he's visited the dazzling moments and the low places on the roads less traveled and is doing sprint triathlons at ninety.

He has a new companion and a smile on his face. His soul has touched those he's met, along with all that competitive drive. Simplify. Do the best you can with what you've got. With so much darkness in the world we could use more light. Lew felt a different call to action completing the Western States One Hundred when he was 54. He's moved towards a freer existence because a strong body makes for a stronger mind. Maybe that's his wish for the world.

CHAPTER 21

THE COSMIC BLENDER

The Rhythm and Patterns of Life—Like many of us, Lew has spent time wondering about the meaning of life and whether there is life in other parts of the universe. Unlike many of us, he wrote a book which addresses the past, present and future of mankind with the possibility of alternative life in the universe, titling it "And Chocolate Shall Lead Us." In his preface he writes "The theory of Dominance was essential for evolution to deliver us to the age of enlightenment. Now, we are at a crossroads; either we abandon Dominance or be destroyed as a species. I attempt, through fiction, to reveal these truths about modern society, for as Shakespeare said, "Many a truth is said in jest." It is my hope that with the help of a 100,000 year old probe from Venus, you can see not only our inevitable self-destruction but also a solution. Through this alien entity, a solution for survival exists with a new set of Ten Commandments and a new vision of a world free of war, poverty and oppression.

The hope for the solution lies within our hearts, and the power to succeed lies in our resolve to abandon dominance." He was fascinated by the movie 2001: A Space Odyssey, and predicts that it won't be long until the world is totally run by Artificial Intelligence. Our brain is not capable of knowing the real world, he says, in terms of alternate reality in what could be alternate universes.

No matter what level Lew seems to be at, he comes across as Everyman. Everyman, no matter where they're at, could probably be more, do more and ask more of the body they're living in. Exercise feeds the brain, and unless you tell your body you are interested in hanging around awhile it will interpret signals you're not sending and take matters into its' own brain. Is it true that truly great athletes get right into the "zone" when needed? The switch of mental focus may enable them to channel all of their abilities onto what they're doing which could be the difference between winning, losing, and actually what level of health/fitness is possible to attain. Not only that, if you're trying to psyche out an opponent, intense focus is one way to do it.

Do the legends in sports achieve it through relentless dedication to their sport(s)? Only they know how relentless they've had to be but one observation suggests that successful training should not be under a lot of continual pressure since it's a long road to the top. The kind of dedication it takes has to be almost ingrained.

Lew's father was a successful baseball player(among many other talents), who played on a championship team in New York. Baseball was one of the first sports Lew started in and had success at, and he played competitively up through the early stages of his professional career. He played short -stop baseball for Cheshire and Delphi University and the US Navy B League team. It's possible to interchange sports quotes for the universal endeavors. As Vince Lombardi has been quoted as saying "winning isn't everything but wanting to win is." Goal setting makes a difference for most goal-oriented people.

But if you never try, that is one of the biggest ways to fail in Lew's philosophy. He's really big on the try part. In Lew's life the rhythms and the patterns are intricate and far-reaching. From climbing the rise of so many mountains, he has had the opportunity to see some great views. And he's been tossed more than once into the cosmic blender. It's given him a better idea about clarity and what is really important in his own life. Maybe to be a great athlete you have to touch on universal themes about life, death, meaning and value.

CHAPTER 22

VELOCITY

Velocity can be defined in a general way as the speed in which an object heads in a specific direction. Point A to Point B, or in Lew's case, to specific points all over the world and then racing. With a voracious, seemingly unsatisfied attitude for burning up the turf. In science and physics he has studied the velocity of matter and come up with systems of measuring specific forms of matter and energy. He's always been blessed with a certain clarity of vision. The young boy who used to mix up formulas in his family home/lab in Woodmere, New York was noticed early on for his focus and brilliance.

"My discoveries came from seeing a need and putting technologies together to accomplish or improve existing methods of doing things. I love science and chemistry. It is like building blocks. Each has a place and if you can see the place you get results," he explains. Conversion of energy fascination started early on just watching his father flip a light switch and getting an explanation. So as he grew the conversion of energy idea got more and more complicated as he challenged himself with bigger questions. As a proactive senior, he's been assembling different kinds of building blocks for conversion of energy in the concept of aging.

He was giving a talk at a national meeting on aging, and everybody was sitting down. He told everyone to standup, and that was the message. Meaning stand up and get going. At another conference he noticed doctors were riding in the escalator when they could have been walking. Exercise and good health are repetitive themes for Lew, themes that go hand in hand with each other. Perhaps it's possible that not enough people have blazed the senior trail as openly as Lew because it's got some scary twists and turns and it's closer to the final place that's so difficult to contemplate. But we need to remember that Lew started analyzing the aging process back when a lot of kids his age were still playing on swing sets.

Somewhere back there in between the industrial revolution, the technological revolution, the internet revolution, TV dinners, fast food, sugars and bad fats, some of us lost pride and knowledge about our animal selves. Really living in our physical bodies, recognizing that the heart after all is a muscle, knowing great things are possible, anything is possible if we just don't surrender too much.

Lew's versatility may not be as widely known as his athletic accomplishments, but he, like many other concerned watchers, would like to see a positive turn in the overall well being of humanity and the planet. So Lew's life has been like an anthem to what is possible. Thanks to many individuals such as Lew, the idea of what is possible with aging is evolving. It takes real leaders to help dip a toe into the deep end. And perhaps the bias against seniors could slowly be turned around again, making good things happen.

Sadly, not all of us will be like Lew. He has been pushing it progressively his whole life as an athlete, and he's studied the effects of exercise, diet and stress. Then he's implemented his ideas, which is probably the most challenging part, since they are not theoretical but take work and discipline. Lew has participated in some of the most grueling and challenging sports possible and at the age of 90 can still do a sprint triathlon and feel perhaps bored. He did a sprint triathlon on his ninetieth birthday but because of COVID it was a virtual race. Ironman is more than a word to those who have earned it.

The responsibility of being a top athlete at ninety has given Lew the motivation to reflect on a lot. He has been called one of the greatest for his age by those who would know. But for all the accolades and accomplishments, honors and praise, what he seems to treasure perhaps the most is how he feels now. And thinks. The NOW is the important thing. Lew seems to be always fresh, he tries not to look back. Maybe he misses the intensity of the high competitive levels, but he's still at the front of the pack in terms of condition. He can't stop, he doesn't want to, he has always loved pushing it so it's all relative. In the process of pushing it, important body glands have been given the message to keep generating their vital stuff. Immune and skeletal systems could be healthier at ninety for Lew than many younger people who have not used it, who slowly ended up losing all of it.

It's never too soon to start planning for the future, for your real health insurance. There's no hidden clauses in the Use It or Lose It guide and there's certainly no pill. The science of laying down the tracks for health are best started way before forty, Lew says in less light-hearted moments. But it better be well in progress by forty or you will fall off the path to a golden senior time.

In earlier days there was a stereotype about taking it easy in your older age. Sure you have to make adjustments. Lew has never taken it easy so he's like a walking poster advertisement against all the negative half-truths about ageing that float around. Maybe there just hasn't been enough courageous leadership or instruction in this field. So the logical question would be, why hasn't there been?

Is it possible that somewhere, buried in the conglomerate subconscious, that we think we will be punished if we eat from the tree of knowledge, of good and evil, that somehow seniors are not entitled to living healthy, active, productive lives? We are definitely being punished the longer we wait to explore the options.

CHAPTER 23

PRIMAL ENERGY

You can feel it when you're around someone who has it. Lew is a beloved figure in the sports world. He's always provided inspiration from giving away rubies in horse racing endurance contests for good condition to continuing to cross the finish line in races, showing multi-generational athletes and non-athletes alike what it's like to go hard, live longer. In 1997 Lew decided to enter the formidable Escape from Alcatraz Triathlon for the sixth time. This time, however, he was also the focus of a profound 3-part BBC documentary on health in seniors, and which helped to explain why it was possible for Lew to continue to perform at such high levels.

He entered the triathlon in the 85-89 age group for the demanding one and a half-mile swim, eighteen-mile bike ride and eight-mile run. When are you OLD, is the question. Lew's idea is that you're really old when you quit dreaming, because you're resigned. It was observed that the 1997 completion of the Escape from Alcatraz Triathlon showed Lew that he still had some races to run. He'd gone through a rare period of gloom after a disappointing Hawaii Ironman, and was considering what his new direction should be when he received a phone call from the secretary of Sheik Nasser bin Hamad Al Khalifa of Bahrain to come participate in a half marathon in the capital city of Bahrain. The invitation was to be the Sheik's guest and participate in the 70.3 Middle East Championship, the idea being that he was an excellent example of what senior athletes can do. Lew got the royal treatment, flew in the royal jet, got picked up in a Mercedes, and the biggest problem he had was having trouble fitting his bike into the Mercedes.The finish of the race took place on the International Circuit Formula One Race section. A good deal of the race ran through the Alareen Wildlife Park. Lew recalls running through the monkey section and thinking it was "pretty cool." Before he left he was introduced to the King because of his incredible success and longevity as a senior athlete. He made the long flight back, and was invited to return within a couple of weeks for another Triathlon, which he did. The Escape from Alcatraz was added to his list and at 87 he joined a large group of other athletes who jumped off of the ferry and headed into shore for the first leg of the race. "If you don't jump off the ferry within the first six minutes or so you're pushed," he observes. "It can be a little scary." The Escape from Alcatraz Race starts off near Alcatraz Island and the swim exit is located adjacent to the Saint Francis Yacht Club off of Marina Blvd. The bike course consists of a lot of hill riding requiring technical skills while the run finishes back at the Marina after traveling through the Presidio and under the Golden Gate Bridge. Lew's pride and competitive spirit have been apparent to all who watch him. He's said frequently that he lives to race, but over a period of time he became aware that he was a representative of hope for many athletes, no matter what the age. As one of the subjects of the BBC's special, it was concluded that Lew is in such great shape because his body is regenerating at a higher level than many just because of pushing it.

He estimates himself that he has raced in over 3,000 race competitions. He's just one of those unusual people who have accomplished so much that it's hard to keep track of. It's not like he spontaneously emerged on the scene and was arbitrarily picked as the poster man. He's been a sportsman and an incredible athlete for a long, long time. It's the versatility in his life that makes him even more fascinating. In his treasure box of memorabilia you could just as easily find a Lockheed Missile & Space Company Certificate of Merit for Invention in the field of Materials Electronics as you could find an Ironman Certificate or family photos.

CHAPTER 24

DEFYING THE ODDS

In 2017 Lew completed the World Championship Ride and Tie finishing eleventh. But doing the extraordinary is what competitive horse people do. Lew was just carrying on a long tradition. Ride and Tie is Lew's favorite sport. Endurance riding, he says, tends to favor small, light people. His strength is running up hills. Ride and Tie is an interesting and complicated dance that involves two humans and a horse at high speeds.

Imagine a 50 mile sprint with another human, a horse, and there is swapping, sometimes at high speed, frequently over rough terrain. I like to let my horse have a loose rein, most of the time, Lew says, because it helps the horse find its way and relax under challenging conditions. Up hills, down hills, crossing water, rocks, narrow trails and the great unknown. As an endurance rider Lew started running alongside his horse as he went for longer and longer distances, wanting to give the horse a break and allow himself to stretch and condition himself.

What's interesting historically is that a challenge issued by the founder of the Tevis Cup Endurance Ride would become a challenge that Lew and his friends would tweak a little later on. Wendall Robie wanted to know if horses of the mid 1950's could handle a tough one hundred mile trail through the High Sierras in around a day. Later on athletes like Lew picked up on that challenge and would eventually run the one hundred mile trail on foot, as it became known as the Western States 100 mile foot race.

In 2015 Lew completed the championship long course near Ashland,

Oregon in Ride and Tie with partner Wash Blakely when he was 85. He used his amazing gelding "Lucky." In 2011 Lew completed the championship long course again on Lucky at the Humboldt Redwoods State Park in California. Lew is ranked seventh in the Ride and Tie Organization with 15 or more championship completions. He's also a member of the thousand-mile club. In this rigorous sport he's had many great horses. One of them, Miss P, has high ranking because she's completed 11 championship races. Lew has also had many great human partners in Ride and Tie but his long time partnership with friend Doug Madsen speaks for itself. They are in Ride and Tie history for 13 championship completions. There are probably few people around who understand the strategy of Ride and Tie and Endurance Riding than Lew. In this excerpt from his book "Endurance Riding, From Beginning to Winning," he explains a little about the psychology of the experience: "...some people are only interested in completion, and that's okay. After all, as we said earlier, the basic premise of endurance riding is "to complete is to win." But there are always people who aren't content to merely ride, they want to race...."

The AERC motto is "to finish is to win."

"I coined that motto and used it in Pacific Northwest Endurance Riding(PNER) and suggested it to the AERC board to raise more money and get more rides involved in the sport and it worked. It is on my Hall of Fame plaque. Also lots more," Lew said.

The Vet Gate was introduced by Lew at the 1976 Oregon 100 ride. Lew reasoned that in order to save the horse there is only one person who can do that--the rider. Riders bringing their horses in at various check -points in good shape were rewarded in a sense. Lew established the GATE concept. When your horse's pulse was down you could go to the gate and be checked by the veterinarian for metabolic condition, soundness, etc. The pulse down to time is a concept almost universally accepted now. Lew also devised the Best Condition (BC) form to encourage uniformity in judging this prestigious award. Previously BC was non-uniform and a very controversial award. Weight and speed were not considered. In 1980, Lew, as chairman of the AERC Best Condition group, wrote a series of articles and received inputs from riders. Then he made up a form to take into account a unified Vet Score, rider weight, and rider speed. He locked the committee in his hotel room until they all agreed to a unified form. Then it was presented to the membership by Lew on January 26th, 1980 at the Reno convention, and adopted by the AERC board. That form has remained approximately the same since that meeting.

CHAPTER 25

COMPETE TO COMPLETE

See you under the full moon—There's always a story in-between stories, there's always personal narrative that has the possibility to become epic. Lew appeared to have burst upon the scene in ultra running but in fact if he hadn't been a champion Endurance Rider and Ride and Tie Champion of considerable repute chances are he wouldn't have appeared to have coasted through so many races on foot. There's nothing like the outside of a horse for the inside of the man. Anyway, in Lew's story, as a little boy, he was fascinated with how energy could be channeled and he loved to ride. For the longest time those two interests have taken him down a mighty road....

Having spent so much time in laboratories working for the Navy and large corporate companies is not related, according to Lew, to embracing the outdoors and athletics. Horse have always been in his life. As a kid he took lessons, worked at a stables, and always had horses in his life. And eventually it was through endurance riding on the Tevis that Lew became acquainted with the Western States one hundred mile trail, though at the time he didn't believe he could do the whole thing on foot.

Lew estimates that he has ridden over ten thousand miles as an endurance rider, but that maybe a low figure because of all the practice miles he's accumulated and it would depend on if the miles from Ride and Tie, billed as the "Thinking Man's Sport," were factored in. Lew's book on successful endurance riding is considered to be one of the bibles of the sport. Endurance riding is timed racing on set mileage where the condition of the horse is extremely important and the rider is obviously responsible for it.

He's also known very well in the rugged sport of Ride and Tie, which combines running, riding, endurance and strategy. To do well you need a great horse and a great partner.

Teams consist of two runners and one horse that complete a course ranging in mileage from 20 to 100 by "leapfrogging one another." That is, one person starts on the horse, the other on foot. The horse travels faster than the runner but it is possible for a really strong team to tire a horse over long distances. Competitors set times where they will pass the horse back at arranged places on the course. There has to be a certain number of passes until the race is completed. Lew last competed in a World Ride and Tie championship set in Oregon when he was 87. Keep in mind that this sport is so tough and demands so many skills that some people half his age couldn't contemplate doing it. Lew's partner was Wash Blakely and they came in 11th. Many were surprised that he competed in the Ride and Tie Championship at Bandit Springs, Oregon in July of 2012 at 82.

His last great endurance horse Lucky lives a charmed life at Lew's Ironman Ranch in Terrebonne, Oregon. They see each other everyday that Lew's home and both seem to enjoy the spectacular view around the place. Lew helped shape Ride and Tie just as he influenced Endurance Riding. His Ride and Tie number 24 makes him one of the very early participants in the sport, since records show him completing his first Ride and Tie World Championship in 1976. Running up hills, running down hills, running on the flatlands--with all that running it would have been surprising not to build up some endurance and speed. Endurance that gave him unique athletic ability.

Because nearly everyday now he runs in the rugged terrain above his house with his wife Karen to do the dance with his old friend anaerobic. His life has been intertwined with the outdoors and horses and mileage for all of his adult life, and preceding it. He entered the extremely competitive world of endurance riding with his second wife Hanne in the mid-sixties.

As he says, they cleaned up whenever they went out, and ultimately helped to shape the sport. They were five times husband and wife National Champions riding over 21,000 miles together and brought their children into it as well.

Lew was responsible for many innovative ideas in the sport at a time when there was a kind of run it and gun it mentality. He accomplished everything he could imagine riding and the marathon running and perhaps that was why Western States pulled him into a whole new world that launched him towards triathlon. Phrases he made popular in endurance riding like "to complete is to win," and "to finish is to win," now resonate in his life in a very special way.

It's all the moments. Running, riding and racing until the sun blends into the moonlight and then back again. Immeasurable moments. Racing with the spirits and against yourself and sometimes definitely against others. Lew has a history of women, races, horses, swimming, biking and science, to name a few, and not necessarily in that order. He's not so much impressed with himself but the collections of moments have come to mean a lot.

Meet me in the moonlight. Lew has raced in five Tevis 100 mile competitions and finished three. It's always held in the summer under a full moon. Long before Lew became known as a solo Ironman he had become part of an exclusive and elite Group of endurance horseman and runners who belonged to the "Triple Cripple Crown Club." The philosophies that have shaped him as a man have also shaped him as a world-renowned athlete in several different sports. High on the list of his treasured qualities is to persist and give it your best shot. This elite club, also known as "The Grand Three," has only 37 members who have dared to take on the three-pronged endurance crown of the West Coast.

The three events include The Tevis Cup(a hundred mile endurance ride), a Championship Ride and Tie Race, and the Western States One Hundred Mile Foot Race, which covers much of the same trail as the Tevis.

The lore of these races has grown into legend over the past few decades as mystified participants contemplate the beauty and the punishment of such grueling races. Originally, the Tevis was started in the mid fifties by noted Horseman Wendall Robie who wanted to know if any horses still existed who could complete the grueling one hundred mile trail from near Squaw Valley to Auburn California in around a day.

Thus the need for a full moon towards the end of July or the beginning of August. What happens at endurance events like this? Maybe it's a kind of catharsis, maybe it's taking a break from the madness of the world, but in-between tough terrain, unpredictable circumstances, and anything that can go wrong, there is the spirit of the challenge. A person can face their demons or their spirituality and come out the better for it. Bonds are nurtured that run deep. It's suggested that there is a kind of spiritual growth that takes place as well as the obvious physical conditioning and toughening. Lew is "extremely proud" of being named with the "really greats" of the endurance world.

What makes great in a person or a horse? In Lew's endurance book he describes in great detail the many attributes that make up a competitive endurance horse. Then there are the more intangible qualities, which he goes on to describe in Chapter One-To Compete is To Win: "Not every horse is capable of finishing an endurance ride, or continuing on to...high mileage totals. An average horse quits when he gets tired. A good horse goes on as long as you ask him to. A great horse goes on to win...It's not easy," he goes on to say, describing the human element. "Sometimes you have to carry on when you're extremely uncomfortable. Perhaps your nose is sun burnt, or you've got blisters where you thought you could never get them. Regardless of the discomforts, endurance riding is fun. It's like marathon running. The sense of accomplishment makes it all worthwhile."

He recalled being in a Ride and Tie around 27 years ago at Eureka CA with over 200 teams of two runners and one horse and he ran with his long-time partner Doug Madsen. "We were in the lead for the prestigious award of 100 years in the saddle and the award was a beautiful hand-tooled leather inscribed chair," Lew explains. "Towards the run for the finish we were ahead and there was a creek crossing and I told Doug "tie at the road above the creek crossing," Lew remembers. He also explains that he is extremely tender footed and cannot run an inch without shoes.

"I am running full speed down across the muddy creek bottom and one of my shoes was sucked off. I had already taken quite a few strides and wondered what to do. I kept going as I knew the horse would be waiting at the road. I get there and NO horse. I had to stumble down the road with one shoe on and one shoe off and the other team passed us and we lost those beautiful chairs....."

So the disappointment was severe along with the tender feet but justice ended up being served, according to Lew. "Three years later at the World Championships held at Bandit Springs in the Ochocos I ran with Doug again and we won the 100 award which happened to be beautiful chairs. I'm looking at one of them right now in my office."

For all the light-hearted moments, and the chilling moments, Lew has also been a behind the scenes supporter in many of the sports he's participated in.

"Lew is very well known in the endurance world, especially in the Northwest Region of AERC(American Endurance Ride Conference), observes Kathleen A. Henkel, current Executive Director of the AERC. "The AERC was incorporated in 1972 and Lew is a lifetime member along with other family members. He was one of the very first members of the AERC Board of Directors responsible for some of AERC's early rules input regarding AERC. Lew and former wife Hanne were very active members along with their children..." she observed.

CHAPTER 26

FIND YOUR WAY— FURTHER DOWN THE TRAIL

It's a priceless spring day in Central Oregon, one that almost makes up for what feels like six months of winter. Lew is running up the long, inclined spine of Grey Butte, an imposing landmark. He's incorporating all of his training methods to complete this slow, gradual push and his dogs are running along for company.

"It's so empowering," I can almost hear him saying. "The body is such an incredible machine."

But finding your way is not always that easy. Many times in a race a competitor can get turned around the wrong way if the directional ribbon or arrow is pointing the wrong way. Is it possible that in some respects that may have happened philosophically to the science of aging?

Lew has courted older age with as much enthusiasm as is possible without indulging in regret or resentment--maybe because he's pushed it just about everyday.

Many of the friendships he's developed over the years have endured. He continues to patent and develop formulas that he finds worthwhile, such as a compound to fight forest fires differently. Karen is "the love of his life" and they have built a relationship which makes it possible to share the joys of everyday life together and stay active.

There's a popular baseball move where an aging scout is contemplating senior adversity and a friend asks him what the problem is. "Old age," he replies.

Questions of aging well can be quite uncomfortable at times. But at the heart of Lew's philosophy is a desire to do his best and carry on his dreams.

There will always be those greater than you and those less than you, he says. All you can hope to do at the end of the day is ask yourself if you did your best. It's when you don't try your best that you lose, come in second or worse.

THE INFINITE CHAPTER

"Lew has not only become an icon in Triathlon for master-ing the skills of the sport but he has become a leader in many ways motivating athletes to strive for more while balancing their lives around friends, family and other priorities.

I hear often that many people aspire to being like Lew, not just at his age but now as people are looking for ways to reinvent themselves around health, fitness and triathlon." Tim Yount—USA Triathlon 30 Year Team USA Manager and USA Triathlon Chief Sport Development Officer.

It's hard to top a complement like that, impossible really. It is safe to say that Lew is known on many different levels for many different reasons around the world based on his accomplishments. But if you have to reduce the essence, which is difficult to do, the resounding adjective might be INSPIRATIONAL.

In some ways Lew is dangerously close to becoming a folk hero tee-tering on the mythological, which we might need. There don't seem to be enough real heroes to go around. Lew has endured and he is real

And he keeps on achieving. Even though he travels in what may seem like elite and prestigious circles, he chooses to come across as Everyman.

Lew's ultra running career gained real attention with the completion of the Western States 100 mile race, a race in which he considers himself to be reborn on many levels, a race which opened his eyes to both limitations and possibilities.

The year 2000 could have ended Lew's racing career with his horrific crash in the cycling portion of the New Zealand Qualifying Triathlon. But as it turns out, what many would consider to be his crowning achievements lay ahead.

It's hard to consider where the turning points come.

But as Lew likes to observe, "many people are good at things but wander off. I persist."

Lew is always beginning.

TRIATHLONS PARTIAL LIST
IRONMAN

Canada

1992	1:19s	6:42b	5:23r	13:25 2nd
1993	1:16	7:10	5:49	14:17:08 2nd
1997	1:26	7:15	5;29	14:12 3/8
2003	1:30:11 Tr1 3:42 6:58:28b Tr2 5:26 5:27:38r 14:05:23 2nd

Arizona

2005	1:38:51	T1-9 7:16:41 T2-4:15, 6:20 42	Tot- 15:32 1st
2006	1:25:32 T1-7:53, b 6:54.23, T-2 7:41, r 7:14:08, Tot- 15:49 1st
2007	1:27:16 T1-8:17 B-7:23, T2-6:36, r-6:14,	Tot 15:24:34
2008	16: ??

Kona

1985		1:37	7:42	6:00	15:19
1989	"	1:25	6:46	5:48	14:00:43
1990	"	1:32	7:52	7:11	16:36
1991	"	1:29	7:24	6:35	15:29
1992	"	1:28	6:55	6:10	14:33
1994	"	1:38	7:24	6:12	15:14:43
1995	"	1:38	8:13	6:33	16:25
1996	"	1:35	8:49	6:26	16:51
1998	"	1:32	7:50	6:19	15:43

1999 1:39:49 7:22 5:38:19 14:52:01 trans1 5:51 trans2 ? WOW
2000 " 1:34:32 7:34:20 5:41:36 14:57:18 tr. 1 4:27 tr.2 2:26 3rd.
2001 " 1:23:05 7:59:51 5:22:15 14:51:43 tr1 3:11 tr 2 3:21 4th.
2002 " 1:25:12 7:15:41 5:56:12 14:43:40 2nd T1 3:46 T2 2:48
2003 " 1:24:59 7:01:16 5:54:02 14:30:34 T1- 5:06 T2 5:09
2004 " 1:34:24 7:46:03 6:13 15:47:39
2005 s 1:47:14 (2.50) T1 6:52, b 7:13:16 (15.5 mph), T2 7:36, r6:36:24 (15.08) **15:51:49**
2006 1:50:11 T1- 5:52, b- 7:25:11 (15:09), T2- 7:38, r- 6:07 (14:01) Tot- **15:36:17 2nd**
2007 1:38:34 T1-7:52, b-7:26, T2-6:31, r-6:27:08 Tot- **15:46:35 2nd**
2008 1:47 7:40:46 r 6:43 16:28:23
2009 S 1:52:12, T1 5:45, B 8:08:54, T2 6:55, R 6:38:44, Tot 16:52:29 4th
      1:52:12 8:08:54 6:38:43 16:52:29 1651 4
2010 S1:50:11 T1 4:05, B- 7:14, T2-6:99, run 6:34:15
Total 15:48:15 1st 80 years old record time

2011 1:57 s swim,7:36 Bike 6:56 run Total 16:45 16:: 116:45:56 1st
2012 2:09 swim 7:44 bike 6:36 run Total 16:45 3rd
2014 DNF
2015 swim 2:02 DNF
2009 LEG
TotAL SWIM   2.4 mi. (1:52:12)   2:57/100m 17673

FIRST BIKE SEGMENT	5.5 mi. (20:55)	15.78 mph
SECOND BIKE SEGMENT	28 mi. (1:32:40)	14.57 mph
THIRD BIKE SEGMENT	59 mi. (2:10:29)	14.25 mph
FOURTH BIKE SEGMENT	88 mi. (2:13:08)	13.07 mph
FINAL BIKE SEGMENT	112 mi. (1:51:42)	12.89 mph
TotAL BIKE	112 mi. (8:08:54)	13.75 mph 1722 4

FIRST RUN SEGMENT	5.2 mi. (1:22:42)	15:54/mile
SECOND RUN SEGMENT	10.3 mi. (1:16:03)	14:54/mile
THIRD RUN SEGMENT	17.6 mi. (1:52:43)	15:26/mile
FOURTH RUN SEGMENT	25.2 mi. (1:56:23)	15:18/mile
FINAL RUN SEGMENT	26.2 mi. (10:52)	10:52/mile
TotAL RUN	26.2 mi. (6:38:43)	15:13/mile 1651 4

TRANSITION	TIME
T1: SWIM-TO-BIKE	5:45
T2: BIKE-TO-RUN	6:55

**BAHRAIN 2015 Dec 5 no swim 6Hr 40 Min 3:17 (18mph) bike 3:13 run
DUBAI 2016 Jan 29 short swim 21:15 bike 3:33 (15.77 mph) run 3:20:21
(15:26 min mi) Tot: 7:25:46**

ST Croix ½ IM 2009
453 LEW HOLLANDERUSA522   7:56:27 M75+1/1 1 S 474 49:31 2:291 433 B
4:00:10 14.01 471 R 3:06:47 14:16
2008 World Championship Clearwater FL
41:05   2:46:00   2:55:00   6:34:41   1224 of 1254   2 of 2
2009

LEG	DISTANCE	PACE	RANK	DIV.POS.
TotAL SWIM	1.2 mi. (41:05)	2:09/100m	1185	2
BIKE SPLIT 1	20.7 mi. (1:02:37)	19.83 mph		
BIKE SPLIT 2	20.3 mi. (57:41)	21.12 mph		
BIKE SPLIT 3	15 mi. (45:42)	19.69 mph		
TotAL BIKE	56 mi. (2:46:00)	20.24 mph		

RUN SPLIT 1	3.5 mi. (47:28)	13:33/mile		
RUN SPLIT 2	3 mi. (39:15)	13:02/mile		
RUN SPLIT 3	3.6 mi. (49:47)	13:52/mile		
RUN SPLIT 4	3 mi. (38:30)	12:50/mile		
TotAL RUN	13.1 mi. (2:55:00)	13:21/mile	1224	2

TRANSITION	TIME
T1: SWIM-TO-BIKE	7:59
T2: BIKE-TO-RUN	4:37

2008 ST Croix ½ IM   S 49:31, B 4:00, R 3:07 Tot 7:56:27

2001 ITU World Championship Fredercia, Denmark 8/4/01 Ironman Distance
1hr 26   T1 7min21   7hr 08 T2 4:29   5hr 13 Total time 14 00 15 1st Gold

2005 ITU   WC Fredericia 8/7/05 1:14 swim 3k, t1 11:39, bike 120k 4:40:20, t2
2:28, 56:18;56:39;57:51;1:00:28 Total time 10:00:40 Gold

2008   ITU Almere Holland WC 4k 2:07 120k bike (chain) 4:08 first 15k run
1:55.29 no finish time on appeal to ITU by USAT and Aust and UK

Florida IM
2000 swim 1:23:23   5:58tr#1 bike 6:30:58 4:33 tr#2   run 5:49:13 Total 13:54:04 1st
2001   1:20 Tot splits 38:44 and 41:49; BIKE 6:18 T2=4:29 ; RUN 2:27;57 1st split
and 2:42:38 2nd split Total run 5:10:34 best ever, Total time 12:58:57 1st CR and PR
2002   13:40:14
2013   1:37 Swim   Tot 15:56
2014   no swim   bike 7:25 run 7:21 Tot 14:57:39

1995 N.Z. 1:30	7:57	5:39 15:16
2000 1:17		16:3? Crashed

Roth Germany Ironman
2000   Swim 1:20:00 tr#1 5:53 Bike 6:36:50 tr#2 3:18 run 5:31 Total 13:37:39

Japan Ironman
1995	1:20	6:55	5:57	14:14
1996	1:17(1:15)	7:28	6:04	14:50:50

WORLD CHAMPIONSHIP SADO JAPAN 1998 3000m s, 106k b, 23k r
s 1:02:15 tr 4:52 (long run) b 3:55:08 tr 2:16 r 2:36:55 Total 7:21:26 GOLD

WORLD CHAMPIONSHIP PERTH AUS. 1997 Olympic dist 65-69 Age Group
5th place 2nd American 30:15 S 1:47 trans 1:24 B :53 tr. 47:22 R Total 2:44:53

WORLD CHAMPIONSHIP Sater Sweden 1999 4k swim, 120k b, 30k r, 7hr
4th place 2nd American

1999 Nationals at St. Jo. 32:56s, 3:15 trans, 1:20:45b, 1:28 trans, 51:59r,
Tot 2:50:21 4th

2000 Nationals at St. Jo. Mi 30:44 s, 2:52 trans, 1:36 b, 1:01 trans, 59:23 r,
3:10:02 2nd (lot of wind and had to run barefooted with bike 2000)

WORLD CHAMPIONSHIP Edmonton Canada 7/01
2001 30:23 S T1 2;02 bike 1:21:15 T2 1 min run 53:16 Total 2:49:07
3rd of 11 Bronze

Alcatraz, Escape 91 shorter run 96 new course

1990	50:43	1:43	3:20	5:54:37
1991	56:03	1:44	2:34	5:14:39
1996 Lewis				
1996				?
2016	1:01	1:38	2:06	5:07
2017		1:54	2:48	4:46

HALF IRONMANS
Boise 1/2 IM
2012 short bike 52.50 s 48:21 B 2:59 r Tot 5:01
2013 51.29 s 3:35 b, 3:15 r Tot 7:51 15.6 mph 14.7 min run
2014 54 s, 3:42 b, 3:14 r, Tot 8:04
2915 54:32 s 3:45:15b 3:35:43 r Tot 8:24:15

St Croix 70.3
2009 Tot 7:56:27 s 49:31, B 4:00:10 R 3:06
2010 7:45:56 49:27 3:51 3:05 (14 min mi)

FAIRMONT CLASSIC Philadelphia 1/2 Ironman
1996 6 hr 14 min

COLUMBIA TRI USTA Championship Olympic dist
1997 32:00s 2:20 tr 1:24:45 b 1:19tr 1:00:01r 3:00:23

Desert Sun 1/2 IM
1998 39:50 (:53) 3:30 bike time 6:58:54 1st out of 6

Florida Disney World ½ IM
2004 54.01 s, (long and no wet suit) T1 2:53, Bike 2:53 19.3m/hr, T2 4:00, run

2:33:45, Total time 6:32:12 2nd

Vineman ½ IM Santa Rosa
2004 8/1   s 43:43 T1 4:28, b 3:00:21, T2 4:46, 2:19, Tot: 6:13:05, 2nd

Clearwater ½ IM World Championship
2008
HOLLANDER, LEW 2/2/2   78/M7596   00:41:05   02:46:00   02:55:00   06:34:41

LONESTAR GALVASTON TX ½ IM
334 Lew Hollander 463 79 1 46:19.90 2:24 04:24.70 1 3:05:30.50
18.1 03:47.30 1 2:59:48.20 13:44 6:59:50.60

2011   Texas Memorial Herman
70.3   0.47swim 3.28 bike 3.13 run Tot 7.38

WILDFLOWER Triathlon 1/2 IM tough course
1991   37:46s 3:41b 2:53r   7:21
1999   2nd place   7:01

Ralph's ½ IM Qualifier Oceanside CA
2004   s 41:49 t-1 7:45 b 3:10:21 t-2 2:22 r 2:20:44   Total   6:22:58 1st
2005   39:22   3:25;!4   2:31:09 T1 8:06 T2 4:18 2nd

CASCADE LAKES 2mi s,54mi b, 13.2mi r,
1985   44   3:39   2:19   6:52
1986   1:08   3:21   7;12
1987   41:58   3:25 2:35   6:42 New course Elk Lake 1.2mi s
1990   37:22 3:16 2:21   6:16
1993   37:23 3:03:18   2:22   6:02

Pacific Crest 1/2 IM Cresent Lake
1997   6:04 short swim 1500 m
1998   41:26   tr 3:34   3:00:34   tr 1:39   2:24   6:11   1st
1999   39:58   tr 4:29   3:09:03   tr 1:23   2:16   6:11:35 1st
2001 Coltus lake   S. 30:25 T1 3:35 B 3:04:48 T2 2:39 R 2:26:06 Tot 6:07:34
2002   "   S 43:51 T1 4:58 B 3:14:57 T2 2:27 R 2:21:39 Tot 6:27:37
2003 S 0:42:41   T1 3:17 B 3:31:43 T2 1:48   R 2:35:14 Tot 6:54:43
2005 1. Lew Hollander   699 75 M 7:22:01 1 0:47:34 517 6:02 3:35:36
527   4:12 528   2:48:36 568 Bend, OR
2006 Olympic 31:36 s, T1 4:17.1:34;32   Bike, T2 2:15, 1:07:34r Tot 3:20:15
2007 77 M 2:54:05 1 0:31:49 203 4:23 1:10:33 121 1:56 137 1:05:24

Pacific Crest Olympic

2009	79	Tot time 3:22:15, S 34:16, T1 4:03, B 1:30:16, T2, R 1:11:27, (226)
2010	80	3:34:34 34:07 4:22 1:33:04 1:34 1:21:17
2011	81	

IDAHO Caldwell 2ks,71.3kb, 22.8kr(14.25mi)

| 1994 | 44:55 | 2:43 | 2:45 | 6:13 |

Troika Spokane

| 1990 | 37:22 | 3:16 | 2:21 | 6:16 |
| 1993 | 37:23 | 3:03:18 | 2:22 | 6:02 |

MEMORIAL HERMANN 70.3 GALVASTON TX

2011 47.23 S, 3:28:50 B, 3:13:00 R, T1 5:00 and T2 4:01 Total 7:38:13

Aluminum Man

1989	3:36
1992	3:25:14
1994	3:15:15
1995	3:29
1996	3:24 (new run course)

1995 New Zealand PIT STOP   1:30:50

1995 New Zealand Nat Ch. 1500, 40k, 10k 3:02:30

1995 New Zealand Refinery 900, 5k 20k   ?

Redmond Triathlon

1983	LEH	1:24:55	Lewis	1:33:17
1984		1:23:43		-
1985		1:23:26		1:33:44
1986		1:21:30		1:27:51
1987		1:23:06		1:22:20
1988		1:21:43		1:13:59
1989		1:21:29		–
1996				
2012				
2013		1:35 Tot 15 s, 39 b 37:39 r 1:35		

Tucson Tri 3.2 run, 825yds swim 12mi bike?

1997	16:01s	39:56b	27:16r

YUMA 1500S?? 10k   30k

1997	14:05	52:33r	1:21:23b	2:28:47

YMCA Eugene Fern Ridge 1mi, 25mi, 10k

1986	39:36	1:16:30	53:30	2:49:33
1985	36:39	1:12	48	2:42:14
				2:44:36
1987	(no water)	1:17	53:30	2:10:39
1987	(Lewis)	1:15	43:32	1:59:03
1988	38:34	1:39	56:23	3:13:59

Ashland NW Championship 4mi.run

1985?	42:45	1:16	38:	3:00:17
1985	41:54	1:57	3:00:23	

USTS Portland Hagg Lake 1mi, 25mi, 10k

1985	46:	1:28	57	3:17
1986	37:12	1:26	58:21	3:06:44
1987	42:28	1:27	1:04	3:19;45
1990				3:09

Hagg Lake Multi Sport

1990	36:05	1:31		1:01	3:09.07
1992	32:01	1:31		1:03	3:07:18
1993	31:55	1:24		56:16	2:52:37
2001	30:32 3:40		1:32:23Bike tr2 1:59	58:18 run	3:06:52 Total

Hagg Lake Nike World Master's

1998	30:35		1:30:07	56:38	2:57:22 GOLD

Hagg Lake USAT Nations 2007

1 945 144 Lew Hollander 77 Bend OR 1 31:42 3:24 3 1:22:13 4:10 1 59:53 1 3:01:20 3:01:20 GOLD

Blue Lakes Tri. 1500m, 23mi, 5mi, ex 89 1000s

1989	17:46	1:14		42	2:15:07
1990	31:45	1:21		52	2:46:17
1991	28:30	1:20		50	2:39:14
1992	27:17	1:18		54	2:39:53
2001	40:41 2:40		4:00 tr1, 1:20:15 Bike 1:36		

tr2, 52:43 run Tot 2:59:16 new course Olympic distance.

Deschutes Dash in river 12 mi bike 5k run
2005 July 24.29 s bike 47:00 run 29.25 Total 1:41:06 bad day
2006   18:05s t1 1:18, bike 48:44 (new course harder) t2 :51, 30:31 run,Tot
1:39:30

USTS San Jose
1987		30:25	2:09	1:07	3:52:13	
1988		37:07	1:59	1:07		3:48:21

OSU Beaver Freezer .5s, 12 b, 3.2 r (?)
1998   9:41 (1:38) 38:52 (0:42) 27:25   1:18 new course record 60+
2001   9:25 (1:30) 42:35 (0:41) 28:09 Total 1:22:20 course record for 70+
           Lewis Mt Bike 8:06 (2:18) 42:33 (1:55) 23:36 Total 1:18:18

HOTV Corvallis
1990		16:20	41:02	24:05	1:24:43
1992		15:48	43:17	26:34	1:28:03
1993	14:46	43:56	26:00	1:27:11	

Canada Championship Calagary
1993		31:13	1:24		55:00	2:51:13

Coeur d'Alene 1500m, 40k, 10k
1993		missed	2:02		58:21	3:00:41

Albany Tri .6s, 12b, 4r (2003 750m swim, 12+ mi bike 5K run
1987		1:25:34
1987	A J Pickard	1:27:22
1991		1:24
1991	Lewis	1:15
1994		1:23
2003		1:27:06

WOSC AJ Tri,
1992	1:42:33
1993	1:46:50

Try A Tri
1987	1:33

Try A Tri Athletic Club 500s, 14mi B, 5K run
2004   s 10:03 57:04 bike, 26:11 run   1:23:14

RACES

Splash and Dash

1988			1:45:08
????			1:29:26
1989	Lewis		1:38
1989			1:51
1990			1:40
1993			1:32:34
1995	Lewis		1:30:44
1995			1:32.04
1998		4th	1:
2001			1:45:18
2004	Lewis 1:43	LEH	1:41
2006			1:49:25
2011	(turned over)		2:04
2012			???
2013			2:09

Cleburne Ironhorse Sprint

2008	bike 18.2 mi/hr run 10.39 min/mi Tot time 1:32:10		
2010	18.6	10:34	1:32:21

2014 Sandman Rio Del Mar 2:19

2014 Santa Cruz International Olympic guess 3:??

Pole Pedal Paddle Bend OR

Once Nancy Cox team and several solo

1993	with Roger	2:11
1994	"	2:04
1996	"	2:14
1997		
1998	"	2:17
1999	"	2:11?
2000	with team	2:01
2001	with Dan Nelson	1:52
2002	with Roger	2:03
2003	"	
2004	"	2:11
2005	"	
2006	2:21:31	

```
2007
2008                    2:20
2009                    2:2?
2011                    2:37
2012   Roger           ???
2013   Jeff Knox   2nd   2:48
2014      "       1st
2015      "       1st
2016   Ken Roadman  1st  77years  3.36.19
2017      "        1st  79       3:31
2018   Ken, Me bike, Roger, Karen Kayak   3:18
2019   6:56 -32   1:08 - 1:04   52 - 3.4  Tot 3:44          "
```

CHAMPIONSHIP RIDE AND TIE

LEW HOLLANDER

1976 Tahoe	Hanne	Bahardy	41st
1978 Davenport	Hanne	Ernie 2MW	18th
1979 Sunriver	Hanne	Ernie	47th
1980 Big Bear CA	Al Paulo	Farmus	21st
1981 Reno Dog Valley NV	Al Paulo	Lew's Big Red	25th
1982 San Jose CA	Doug	Sadie	89th
1983 Eureka CA	Doug	Mis P	15th
1984 Park City UT	Doug	Haysue	16th
1985 Foresthills CA	Doug	Haysue	19th
1986 Big Creek CA	Doug	Lightning	34th
1987 Big Creek	Doug	Haysue	23rd
1988 Alturas CA	Doug	Wendy?	27th
1990 Trinidad CA	Doug	Mis P	31
1991 Taylorsville CA	Doug	Mis P	1st 100 years in the saddle
1992 Davenport CA	Doug	Mis P	28th
1994 Taylorsville CA	Doug	Mis P	48th (Doug ran past P)
1995 Sun Valley ID	Lewis III	Mis P	28th
1996 Davenport CA	Lewis III	Mis P	55th
1997 Ft Bragg, CA	Sid	Mis P	13th
1998 Donner CA	Sid	Mis P	13th
2001 Truckee CA	Sid	Mis P	11th
2002 Truckee CA	Doug	Mis P	12th
2003 Truckee CA	Dave Wagner Mis P		12th 5 hours 12 min
2004 Ft Bragg	Debbie Wagner Nick		10th
2010 Mt Adams WA	Melissa Queen Najim		13th
2011 Humbolt CA	Doug	Najim	??
2012 Bandit Springs OR	Doug	Suzzie Horse	23
2015 Southern Oregon	Wash Blakley	Lucky	11th

LEWIS HOLLANDER III

1983	Nance	Nance horse	99th (10 and 11 years old

youngest team to have completed the Championship race. 99th out of over 200 teams)

1995 Sun Valley	Lewis III	Mis P	28th
1996 Davenport	Lewis III	Mis P	55th
2004 Ft. Bragg	Dave Wagner Mis P		8th

BIATHLONS: RUN-BIKE-RUN

Summer Games
1991? hits 5p 2s   19:38

Firecracker Portland
1991	21:47	57:18	23:39	1:42:44
1992	22:43	49:52	25:35	1:38:10

Mazama
1991		22:52	59:07	26:20	1:48:19	
1991	Lewis	18:50	49:33	20:31	1:28:54	
1997		24:01	1:02	25:12	1:51:46	windy and rain
1999		24:11	59:35	25:23	1:51:07	

RoseFest Tanisbourne
1990	22:53	1:04	26:13	1:53:46
1991	22:33	56:12	26:40	1:45:25
1992	17:52*	1:00:53	24:59	1:43:46
1993	23:19	1:01:24	25:40	1:50:23
1994	23:35	1:01:48	25:13	1:50:36
1999	24:			2:00:

Midsummer
1989	21:16	1:05	24:37	1:51:01
1991	22:24	56:06	23:20	1:41:50

Bend Biathlon 5k r, 30k b, 5k r up Mt B
1995   25:?   1:58

Road Warrior Kan-Nee-Ta 22mi, b; 10k r
1999   54 run 2:20

Fresh Air Sports Duathlon series
7/13/05	bike 42:22	run 30:37	tot 1:12:59
7/27/05	42:57	33:53	1:16:50
6/29/06	42:13 blue bike	run 34:26	1:16:39

Bend Bike and Sport Time Trials
7-12-06   42:29 silver bike

Sunrise to Summit Duathlon Bike Bend to Mt B run to Summit
2006 9/2/06	3:07	estimate bike split	1:37
2007 9/1/07	3:02	bike	1:32

MARATHONS

Devils Lake to Lava Camp
1995 Aug   6 hours ....25 mi.

Hells Canyon Runs 31 River Mi 4/21/90
1st   8:23   with Rob DeVellice

Tucson Marathon
1996............................4:20
1999............................3:50

Las Vegas 5K 21:00

Seattle Marathon
1995............................4:13:29

Cal International Marathon
1988............................4:01:37
1991............................3:55:36
1993............................4:01
1997............................4:08

Portland Marathon
1978............................4:48
1979............................4:18
1982............................3:29:38
1983............................? medal
1984............................3:51:02
1986............................4:50
1987............................4:09:54
1988............................4:00
1989............................4:01
1990............................4:56:12
1991............................4:28:49
1994............................4:13
1996............................4:10

San Francisco Marathon
1980............................4:22:19

San Diego Marathon
1999............................4:24
2000............................4:17
2001............................4:14 1st
2002 ....4:12:31 2nd

Boston
1983............................3:51

New York
1980............................3:52
1983............................3:17:30

Montreal
1981............................4:21

Bidwell, Chico
1979............................4:18

Skagget 50 mi Ultra
1982............................9:53:54

Western States 100 mi
1984............................28:52

American River 50 miles
1993............................11:15

McKenzie River 50 miles
1993............................10:49

ABOUT THE AUTHOR DANA BURNETT

Dana Burnett knew early on that she wanted to be a writer. She has been published all over the West Coast specializing in human interest, sports and horse-related stories. She has published her own coming of age youth adventure and continues to use writing as a way to combine adventure, information, awareness and love.

Sports and exercise have always been an important part of her life.

Dana has written about a diverse collection of topics over the years and has interviewed prominent actors, musicians and politicians. She has combined a life-long love of horses with writing and work and has had many notable successes in those areas. She knows that getting a worthwhile story always takes a lot of work and a little risk, and she's been working at it for over forty years. Dana has had a handful of truly great teachers over the years who encouraged her and always illustrated ideals with the way they lived their own lives.

CPSIA information can be obtained
at www.ICGtesting.com
Printed in the USA
LVHW070024230622
721878LV00010B/350